T0091482

Intelligent Information Systems – Vol. 5

Adaptive Micro Learning
Using Fragmented Time to Learn

INTELLIGENT INFORMATION SYSTEMS

ISSN: 1793-4990

Series Editors: Da Ruan *(Belgian Nuclear Research Centre (SCK.CEN) &
Ghent University, Belgium)*
Jie Lu *(University of Technology, Sdyney, Australia)*

Intelligent Information Systems – Vol. 5

Adaptive Micro Learning
Using Fragmented Time to Learn

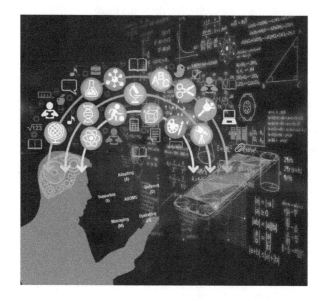

Geng Sun
Jun Shen
Jiayin Lin

University of Wollongong, Australia

World Scientific

EW JERSEY · LONDON · SINGAPORE · BEIJING · SHANGHAI · HONG KONG · TAIPEI · CHENNAI · TOKYO

Published by

World Scientific Publishing Co. Pte. Ltd.

5 Toh Tuck Link, Singapore 596224

USA office: 27 Warren Street, Suite 401-402, Hackensack, NJ 07601

UK office: 57 Shelton Street, Covent Garden, London WC2H 9HE

British Library Cataloguing-in-Publication Data
A catalogue record for this book is available from the British Library.

Intelligent Information Systems — Vol. 5
ADAPTIVE MICRO LEARNING
Using Fragmented Time to Learn

ISBN 978-981-120-745-7

For any available supplementary material, please visit
https://www.worldscienti ic.com/worldscibooks/10.1142/11477#t=suppl

Contents

Chapter 1

Introduction

1.1 Background

1.1.1. *Background*

With the rapid growth of technology, the learning patterns become diverse, and they are no longer solely restricted in the classroom and with paper-printed textbooks. In other words, the learning activities can take place in distance empowered by multiple types of equipment. The distance learning is usually to expand its impact with the assistance of electronic means, simplifying the method of information delivery and deriving new fields of teaching approach. Education providers are showing increasing interests in releasing their learning resources online in the digital form, including text, image, audio, video, and so on. Therefore, learners can utilize the electronic learning (e-learning) extensively to participate in learning activities and access learning contents on their own schedule. Therein, learners are given freedom to be self-paced and able to make their own decisions to slow down or speed up their learning rate of progress as needed. The development of e-learning does not replace the traditional on-campus or class-based learning, but it eases the way of accessing to learning resources by leveraging advanced learning technologies, and to improve them by accommodating multiple learning styles using a variety of teaching methods and delivery mechanisms adapted to different learners. Hence, the adoption of e-learning can offer learners the 24hour/7day learning experience and eliminate the geographical barriers in some extent.

The significant development of e-learning can be viewed from two perspectives. Firstly, the learning opportunities can be gained anytime and anywhere through the use of mobile devices, provided that wireless network is well achievable. Among all types of learning modes in e-learning, mobile learning (m-learning) is rising remarkably, from which learners are given more freedom to have learning activities wherever they are and whenever they want. Consequently, they are no longer required to keep sitting in front of a computer, desktop or fixed device, while they can carry portable devices to enjoy the convenience in the mobile environment.

An eye-catching phenomenon of m-learning is that the fragmented pieces of time can be made good use. In addition, with the widespread use of mobile devices, people are taking advantage of smart phones and tablets to engage in online learning, which is termed as "micro learning". Micro learning is a type of short-term learning involving activities based on small learning units. It is based on the assumption that a short time span is needed to complete a relevant learning task. It requires not only the learning task to be fragmented, but also that it to be completed (rather than being left unfinished halfway). In contemporary e-society, micro learning pertains to small pieces of knowledge delivered through open education resources (Kovachev et al. 2012). It is a major learning channel in mobile environment and is becoming popular with next-generation learners who learn on the move, with easy access to the 'cloud' or Internet of Things (Bruck et al., 2012; Hug & Lindner, 2005). As a result, most open education resources (OER) providers have promptly released their mobile apps on mainstream mobile devices and operation systems (e.g., iOS, Android) and adapted their Webpages to appropriate screen size and operational mode of mobile devices to enable more convenient use for learners.

Secondly, a massive amount of learning resources has been made open to public. Academics have been sharing digital content since the early days of computing (Land & McAndrew, 2010). Online learning through OER is one of the latest technologies in the field of education. It provides an open network-based model to achieve free or low-cost learning for any age group. It has become an important resource base for teachers and students around the world. In 2001, MIT, as a pilot, firstly launched Open Course Ware (OCW), with the aim of publishing all its courseware on the Web, and with licenses which allow the use, modification, and redistribution of published courseware. Since then, many other universities have joined the movement of making their courseware materials open. The promotion of OER benefits learners to access materials directly and learn from them, and allows educators to use materials directly or with modifications in their own teaching (Liyanaguanawardena et al., 2013). Through OER, anyone from any background with any level of expertise is given equal opportunity to attend courses and have access to educational contents and knowledge that they otherwise could not afford. In particular, millions of people are currently participating in the virtual classroom of the Massive Open Online Course (MOOC). Indeed, the number of students enrolled in a single course at the same time could be as high as tens of thousands (Souza & Amaral, 2014). As more and more universities and other educational institutions offer online access to their courses, open learning gains wider popularity in adult education, particularly in tertiary and vocational education.

1.1.2. *State of Research Problem*

The use of mobile devices for open online courses poses additional challenges for the adaptive delivery of learning contents. In a m-learning environment, learners can use their mobile device to access any learning content from the Internet. They have full control of the time and location of their learning; they are not limited by a class timetable or classroom location. Learners are also able to choose the content they want to learn; they do not have to learn what the teacher has prepared and scheduled for that class in advance. Despite the numerous advantage of m-learning, until recently the practicality of m-learning has been limited due to the quality of the supporting technologies and the overloaded learning contents available to them. On the other hand, people make use of their surrounding environment through interactions with others; they interpret their current context and react to it. For example, when students interact with peers, they automatically observe their peers' tones of voice and respond in an appropriate manner. Devices such as mobile phones are not able to interpret the surrounding context in the same way as human do in an interactive environment. These types of devices cannot make a full usage of the available information in a transparent way; therefore, the context information must be explicitly supplied to these devices to allow the devices to respond appropriately (Sharples et al., 2009). Particularly in m-learning applications, contextual and personal characteristics have a strong impact on each other, i.e. personal characteristics determine a learner's behaviour and the behaviour determines the context. The concept of being context-aware is composed of two elements: personalization related to the learner, and automatic customisation related to the adaptation process. Personalisation related to the learner means that the system knows about the learner and provides tailored contents adaptively towards to the learner's needs (Al-Hmouz et al., 2012, Xu et al., 2014).

Automatic customization means that the system creates a model for the learner in an automatic way, based on machine learning mechanisms, to suit the learner's situations and needs. Although the personalized learning resources customization have been discussed over years (Zhuhadar &Nasraoui, 2008), the open learning mode is too new to be involved in this research effort. Thus, few personalized learning deliveries have combined characteristics of open learning. An individual learner's specific needs can vary significantly in open learning, which are normally different from traditional learning. Few research has been done in the field of enhancing open learning experience by taking advantage of learner modelling and educational computing techniques.

The delivery effectiveness of OERs to learners in diverse learning environments remains challenging. Plenty of these OER were of limited use, since they were built as specific parts of some larger educational experience within specific educational framework (Adames et al., 2013). On mobile platforms, learners' attention spans are often limited to 15 minutes, as they frequently interrupt their learning activities and switch their attention to other activities (Stockwell, 2008). Studies on MOOC have shown that online courses are currently suffering from low completion rates. In addition, as one of the major MOOC providers, edX found that the videos lasting less than 6 minutes are more attractive, as student engagement drops sharply after 6 minutes (Hylen et al., 2012; Guo et al., 2014). Most learners who enrol in online courses eventually drop out for a variety of reasons (Nawrot & Doucet, 2014). As the research and development of OERs is still in its infancy, there are evidently many research gaps concerning how to improve its learning mechanisms, such as providing more effective learning platforms and learning support services, so as to enable easier access and better experiences for both service providers and learners.

Moreover, studies on learning resources adaption have not been extended to micro learning scenarios, and they have not taken into account the length or scale of learning resources or learners' spans of time availability. Fragmented learning with mobile devices requires learners' concentration and reflection. However, being on the move is fraught with unpredictable situations and distractions. This leaves mobile learners with a highly distracted, highly fragmented learning experience. In addition, studies indicate that personality and learning styles play significant roles in influencing academic achievement (Daradoumins et al., 2013). Learners may be at their wits end to choose which courses to study initially, or subsequently when there are many options to consider. There are high probabilities that they cannot access the most appropriate sets of micro OER, which can affect their achievement of satisfactory outcomes even when they have expended substantial time. In the current open learning environment, learning resources are often divided and packaged by education providers or courses lecturers. This approach lacks the flexibility needed to fit a specific learner's learning style, progress, and availability. Quite often, learners need to squeeze their time to accomplish those learning activities because they are taking the content passively. Our colleagues' pilot work developed an adaptive mobile learning system prototype, but it still lacks a mechanism to adjust those courses already in-progress (Al-Hmouz et al., 2010), where students need to prepare themselves with a schedule and plan their time carefully over a comparatively long period, without personal guidance. Therefore, bringing micro learning into open learning environment exposes a significant research gap to fill.

The terms micro learning through OER and micro open learning will be used interchangeably in the rest of this book.

1.2 Research Objectives

Effective micro content delivery is one of the major barriers to be overcome by course instructors or deliverers in adapting their previous teaching strategies to micro learning environments (Sun & Shen, 2014). Therefore, this book aims to investigate how smarter micro learning systems can help learners to take advantage of fragmented time they spend on mobile devices in accessing OER.

In regards to covering the current research gap in tailoring personalized micro OER and enabling easier access and better experience for both service providers and learners, this book aims to address a variety of issues in the adaptive micro open learning, considered through the micro open learning framework design, personalized learner model construction oriented to micro open learning, educational data mining and learning analytics (EDM and LA) strategic design, semantic learner and micro OER profiling, agile solution for cold start problem. This book introduces a novel approach towards providing adaptive OERs, which are fragmented pieces tailored to fulfil the requirement of carrying out micro learning.

1.3 Contribution of the Book

As a result of the proposed objectives, the contributions of this book can be highlighted as bellows:

- A system framework is developed in terms of the service-oriented architecture (SOA). The system, Micro Learning as a Service (MLaaS) adopts both offline and online computation domain to work in conjunction so as to improve the performance on learning resource adaption.
- We propose a comprehensive learner model that allows the system to consider individual learning styles, learner's contexts, application capabilities, and teaching materials structure, leading to a customization of the type and delivery format of learning information in response to the user.
- A knowledge base that fills the gap of formal OER structuring, description, and inference is constructed. A detailed EDM and LA

strategy is scheduled with regards to on-campus learning data sources and open learning data ('big data') sources.

- A solution is provided for organizing online computation in MLaaS and a heuristic approach for addressing cold start problem in the recommendation of micro OERs. This solution is empirically evaluated to prove its feasibility.

1.4 Outline of the Book

This book consists of three sections, in a sequential order:

- The theoretical aspects of the research, which will be presented in the Chapter 2, 3, 4, and 5.
- The practical aspects of the research, which will be presented in the Chapter 6 and 7.
- The conclusion part of the research and suggestions for further research, which will be presented in the Chapter 9.

The rest of this book is organized as follows:

The Chapter 2 will introduce the basic principle of this research, including terminology and a literature review. It will start from a comprehensive examination over the literature on distance learning and its development, namely the move from e-learning to mobile learning. Next, the impact brought by the open learning and OERs. The feasibility of embracing the micro learning with the open learning will be discussed. This chapter emphasises the advantage of micro open learning and highlight the inspiration to improve its current way of delivery. Techniques that will be applied in the research include learner modelling, EDM and LA, and big data.

The overall design of the research will be roll out in the Chapter 3. The research background will be stated along with our pilot study. Motivated by this, the research purpose will be demonstrated with example scenarios, where ideally the adaptive micro learning activities can be organized. In the last section of the Chapter 3, a framework of MLaaS will be presented to depict the process of adapting micro OERs to satisfy individual learner's needs and context. MLaaS's functions will be jointly empowered by the online and offline computation domains.

Typically, there are a number of factors that impact the learning experience and outcomes. In Chapter 4 we will conceptually build a comprehensive learner model oriented to the micro open learning. Features that can play roles in the entire process of micro open learning will be selected, from both internal and external sides. The internal factors can intellectually or non-intellectually reflect learners' learning behaviours. In addition, from the item perspective, we will give an overview of the micro learning content (i.e. micro OERs). The mechanism to categorize and customize micro OERs will be illustrated, followed by the measurement standard.

Based on Chapters 3 and 4, the semantic knowledge base construction will be conducted in the Chapter 5, using a top-down approach. Its pattern level at the top will have the augmented ontologies for micro OERs and learners, respectively, which will be represented by conceptual graphs. Data sources at the bottom level will be processed in terms of a EDM and LA based strategy, which is to understand micro learning patterns and rules, from the both on-campus data and open learning data perspective, and to support the decision-making process of the micro OER recommendation system.

To kick off the practical aspect of this book, the Chapter 6 will spread out the details of the online computation of the MLaaS. The online computation aims to evidently support the first decision-making process of micro learning adaption and delivery. First of all, a solution to tackle the famous cold start problem will be presented as the main contribution of this chapter. A lightweight learner-micro OER profile will be built on top of the comprehensive learner model in order to act on the cost start condition and fast response. Subsequently, it will also look for the way to insert newly published micro OERs into well-established learning paths and the real-time updating of comprehensive learner models.

The Chapter 7 will provide the empirical evaluation results for the proposed computation approach. The experiments will be operated based on a series of simulations in which heuristic algorithms will be selected and optimized to realize the computation process. The system implementation will also be involved in this chapter.

The Chapter 8 will conclude this book and provide suggestions for future research.

Chapter 2

Literature Review

As a new phenomenon emerging in recent years, micro open learning has been attached great significance and attracted interests from both researchers and developers. The success of adaptive micro open learning is closely related to the proper utilization of a combination of topics from both technical and educational perspectives. In this chapter, we will go through relevant literature in the computer science, information technology, data science and pedagogy areas. Firstly, literature in the areas of mobile learning and micro learning will be reviewed in the Section 2.1. Then the background and development of open learning and open educational resources will be discussed in the Section 2.2. Next, the combination of the both phenomenally new learning trends, micro (learning and) open learning (i.e. micro learning over OERs) will be examined through its benefits and research gaps; lastly, we will also investigate studies over the learner modelling, and educational data mining (EDM) and learning analytics (LA) in the Section 2.4.

2.1 Mobile Learning and Micro Learning

2.1.1. *Distance Learning and Electronic Learning*

Distance learning enlarges the concept that learning activities have to be physically performed in a definitive place, often a classroom. Hence, in the context of distance learning, teachers and learners are usually isolated by time and location; meanwhile, learners and their classmates, or teammates are virtually distributed. This type of learning approach gives the teachers freedom to arrange their schedule, and allows learners to work on their learning contents in their preferred time. In terms of these, more education opportunities are offered to learners whom are unable to attend traditional classroom due to disabilities, sickness, whom want to engage in advanced study apart from full-time work, and whom are willing to but far away from their ideal education institution, such as learners in developing countries (Woods et al., 2011).

The central idea of the distance learning is the delivery of knowledge, which is usually realized by the aid of some technologies and communication tools. For example, in the earliest form of distance learning, teaching by correspondence through post is commonly adopted. Some open universities or open course providers often make use of the television education and videoconference in the twentieth century. Researchers determined this phenomenon as the rudiment of electronic learning (e-learning).

With the rapid development of Internet technologies, e-learning, which is the acquisition and use of knowledge distributed and facilitated primarily by electronic means is gradually playing an important role in pedagogy (Wentling et al., 2000). Urdan and Weggen (2000) defined e-learning as "the delivery of content via all electronic media, including the Internet, intranets, extranets, satellite broadcast, audio/video tape, interactive TV, and CDROM."

Discussion of the e-learning's features can be widely found in literature. Some typical points of view are summarized as follows:

- For distance learning supported by e-learning, teachers and learners are no longer required at the same location, while in-classroom learning experience is also involved by taking electronic equipment as assistance.
- E-learning can be self-paced or instructor-led. Many education institutions have made learning resources readily available to learners, including lecture videotapes, lecture notes, lecture slides, reference books, etc. That is to say, learners can access those by themselves with their freedom and preference (Bates and Poole, 2003). The commencement and termination of learning activities are in their own hands, and they decide which resources they want to subscribe, what aspects they should emphasize and how long each learning stage should take. To the contrary, the teachers' roles in e-learning can be simplified, as making the guidance about related subjects, pointing out

the right learning direction, sharing experiences and answering questions when learners are confused (OCED, 2005).

• The activities in e-learning can be either synchronous or asynchronous. On the one hand, two or more participants can exchange their ideas or information within the same period, which is typically supported by chat room, instant message software and video communication equipment. On the other hand, with the mature Web 2.0 technology, asynchronous learning activities, which are by the aids of blogs, Wikis, discussion boards, etc., become frequently used in recent years. Hence, participants are no longer required to respond as soon as they receive information, without the dependency of other participants' involvement at the same time.

There are many e-learning systems, also known as learning management systems (LMSs), which are software applications for documentation, tracking, reporting, and the delivery and administration of education courses or training programs. Most LMSs are Web-based which can facilitate access to learning content and expand the usage range. General learning contents provided in LMSs are in the form of text, image, animation, streaming video and audio.

2.1.2. *Mobile Learning*

Mobile learning (m-learning) emerged as a brand-new trend of e-learning with the evolution of wireless technologies and wide use of mobile devices (Sharple et al., 2002).

The major difference between these two types of distance learning is that, e-learning is generally carried out in front of a computer or a fixed device, while m-learning can take place at any location (Sharma and Kitchens, 2004). For this reason, learners are able to have m-learning wherever they are and whenever they want. Learning activities happening on campus, at home or outside school facilities can be integrated into mobile education environment (Kim et al., 2006). In addition, a trend in m-learning is that the learners are using mobile devices and actually in movements while the teachers may use multiple types of equipment other than mobile devices and be located in fixed places (Vanska, 2004).

Koole et al. (2010) stated that the m-learning promotes the utility of distance learning. Compared to distance learning, m-learning has several additional features that should be considered for the delivery of a high-quality education experience:

- Accessibility: it is primary for m-learning. The study environment is in movement and all study resources and learners are mobile. The learning activity cannot be broken off if the learning space-time is changed. Learners are not restricted by time and location (Attewell, 2005).

- Personalization: In the m-learning environment, each individual learner's condition can be extraordinarily hybrid and complex, such as different bandwidths and network conditions varying from time to time. Also, their mobile devices may have various screen sizes and typing methods. Personalization is the characteristic that different individual learning needs and learning properties are adapted to different learners (Sharma and Kitchens, 2004). It should also focus on delivering the appropriate contents to study in a particular way. Some researchers addressed that the m-learning should be context-aware to adapt learners in different conditions (Economides, 2008; Negella and Govindarajulu, 2008; Zervas, Ardila et al., 2011).

- Convenience: Due to the limited memory and processing capabilities, commonly learners use mobile devices to access m-learning resources via thin client or web browser; these portable devices should well enable network connectivity, rapid setup and equipment reusing. The readability of content, operability of interface and learners' satisfaction should be also taken into consideration (Georigiev, Georigiev et al., 2004).

- Interactivity: There are three types of interactions in the m-learning: learner to learner, leaner to teacher and learner to content (Koole, Mcquilkin, et al. 2010). Each of these three interactions is expected to be done hassle-free, regardless the time and location.

Relatively, traditional m-learning more focuses on the content delivery, but lacks the ability to process assessment and feed back to LMSs. However, along with the booming of technologies, the context of m-learning evolves significantly which is far more advanced and complicated than five years ago. Wherein, obvious changes can be concluded to the widespread use of intelligent equipment and the upgrade of infrastructure.

Exemplified by the smart phone and tablet, the intelligent equipment improves the user experience of m-learning by offering the full-touch-screen and integrated computing capability. Due to their gradually complete functions, they are replacing the use of PDA, feature (non-smart) phone, portable media player and e-reader. To some extent, the limited screen and typing method of traditional mobile device are promoted. By using these, learners have more freedom to customize and download the learning materials based on their individual mobile operation systems. Meanwhile, more and more applications and lightweight applications (apps) are released in the education area, as well as the e-book can be read on a broad variety of mobile operation systems.

The problem caused by phone signals is somehow remitted by the advantages high-speed network (4G, 3G, GPRS and Wi-Fi etc). Web contents of LMS system should fit to the screen size of mobile devices, on which the online audio and video can also be played smoothly. In addition, the communication approaches in the m-learning environment become abundant with the support of upgraded infrastructure. Ting (2005) summarized that there were three types of communication approach in m-learning before the year of 2006: voice communication (e.g. phone call), short text message and communication on internet (e.g. Online chat and email), and the first two are served by communication-operation corporations (e.g. telephone companies) and charge in terms of phone bills. Since 2006, much more online tools and apps have been developed to support instant communication. The voice communication and short text message, even in a group format, are feasible to be realized and can be easily achieved through the Internet. In addition, learners are able to use multimedia-based message to communicate among each other, so that they are only billed by the consumption of the network quota rather than the phone usage, or even for free when Wi-Fi network is well available.

The development of m-learning neither intends to completely replace traditional distance learning, nor is about to resize and restrain the course into pocket devices. However, it dedicates to enhance distance learning with the power of wireless network, and augments the formal knowledge delivery (Ting, 2005). Hence, it is believed that some new trends raised by m-learning will arrive in the near future, which can be concluded as:

- More and more mobile devices are employed into classroom as supplements of traditional learning resources. This means can augment the formal learning so as to reach a scene of blended learning (Vaughan, 2010). For example, m-learning may be used to introduce some chapters of a course while the rest is conducted in real face-to-face education (Mellow, 2005).

- Online courses delivered through the LMSs are dramatically exploding, giving learners more choices to participate in on demand delivery. They can use mobile devices to browser learning resources, and accomplish, upload and check assignments, by one-stop service, which is more practical to arrange the education process.

- The e-book gradually replaces the traditional paper-printed textbook. The e-book's content is easy to update. Teachers and learners benefit from this convenience so as to be not out-dated (Zawacki-Richte et al., 2009).

- Multimedia-based content is increasingly blended in teaching materials, which gets knowledge passed on in creative and vivid ways. The learning experience changes to non-baldness.

- It becomes very common that learning for multiple times with each learning time shortened. That is to say, learners are able to utilize more fragmented pieces of time to learn, when they are queuing up, on the way or at the time slot of other events, and so on.

- M-learning can be simultaneously combined with social network to link learners, raise discussions and spread out information, from which the information-push technology guarantees that learners who are offline or in phone-signal-lacked areas never miss a message.

- Online collaborative learning gains its popularity, which engages numbers of learners to join for working towards common goals.

There were various drawbacks of mobile learning in the past decade. For example, learning resources for non-mobile devices cannot be directly adapted to mobile devices due to their indeterminacies of context (e.g. unpredictable network bandwidth), and specificities (e.g. different operation systems). Inspired by these, educational experts suggested that a key catalyst for m-learning to thrive is the services oriented and cloud computing paradigms, which harness economic benefits of large scale distributed systems, and computing resources are seamlessly integrated across geographical boundaries (Sarrab et al., 2015). The prosperities of m-learning and mobile service are usually discussed together because they have shared a lot of common features, such as location-based specificity (Dinh et al., 2011). This suggests that m-learning and mobile service can be facilitated mutually. We will discuss this new trend of m-learning in the next section.

2.1.3. *Mobile Cloud-based Learning*

The traditional m-learning proceeding without cloud computing suffered from some disadvantages, they can be concluded as the following two aspects:

- For education providers, administers and teachers, the novel deployment and management for LMSs to support m-learning functions pose huge difficulty to them. Due to the variety of user requirements, contents in the m-learning systems are preferably to be user-defined, while how to choose and configure the extended components of LMSs is also not easy so that teachers and administers have to get trained otherwise they cannot adapt to the changeability of component configuration which is unique to each component. On the other hand, the traditional LMSs are defective in large-scale deployment. In research and implementation of m-learning, deployment from single site to provide overall services is generally centralized in the school level. However, this traditional deployment cannot meet the requirement of granularities of several levels distinguished by scales. According to the coarse granularity, equipment performance and security of m-learning would suffer from constraints and drawbacks root in providing services from the region level or even the country level. To the contrary, in terms of the fine granularities, school, class and individual teacher require independent utility of m-learning by the aspect of personalization. Furthermore, quick deployment of the LMS is also an issue (Orr, 2010). From the commencement to the normal operation, it takes a long time to complete network configuration, system software configuration, and also configuration for m-learning context and content. Additionally, some LMSs are open-source software that lack guide documentations and subsequent technical support. For example, the famous Moodle[a] and Bodington[b]. In this case, once any problem occurs on the open-source m-learning system, general teachers and administers can face difficulty in solving the problem without aid from professional technicians. Lastly, the cost is always the unavoidable issue, which involves the charges of hardware, software, collocation, network renting and electricity. Professional technicians are organized for maintenance and repairing of m-learning system, the expenditure for whom cannot be ignored as well. The repetition of m-learning deployment in each school is deemed as a large waste of resources (Cobcroft et al., 2006).

- For learners, although latest processors that empower mobile devices have been updated to high-speed, the power consumption still fails to meet the requirements of current m-learning. It can be oppugned about the process efficiency and reaction rate when using mobile devices to run a complicated m-learning system. The highly centralized operation by mobile processors should also be enabled by a high- power battery, which is not fully settled in current products. The shortcoming on heat dissipation of mobile devices may also make leaners unsatisfied. Moreover, in the traditional mode of m-learning, teachers arrange the learning content and design the learning process according to the syllabuses, whose knowledge hierarchies and the syllabuses limit the depth and breadth in some degrees. An obvious result is that how much the learners can gain is closely related to how much the teachers have imparted. Additionally, the formation of learner clusters is basically in charge of the education provider and teacher, who are in control of the structure of learners, the organization of learning content, the rollout of strategy and path of

---

[a] moodle.org

[b] elframework.org/projects/tall/bodington/view.html

learning in certain extents. This causes that the interaction and knowledge sharing are somewhat in a very local range and limited.

Nevertheless, all of the above issues are feasible to be tackled in the coming of a new trend, namely embracing mobile learning with mobile cloud computing. Consequently, with the solutions that either migrating current LMSs to cloud or directly developing them on the cloud, learners can effortlessly learn through mobile devices (Sultan, 2010). This is a novel way of m-learning, namely mobile cloud-based learning.

By leveraging the mobile cloud-based learning, the primary advantage is the lower cost. The requirement for hardware and software is significantly reduced. In particular, since all of the data storage and processing are in the cloud side, the limited processor capacity and memory size of mobile devices are no longer bottlenecks for a pleasant m-learning experience. Hence, the learners can only use mobile devices, which only have to run a browser and connect to the wireless network, for input and output of data.

Similarly, education providers and administers no longer need to own and set-up high-performance services by themselves, without caring about the background of LMSs running. The expenditure of purchasing and upgrading hardware can be lowered. Not only is the fast deployment of LMS well enabled by mobile cloud computing, but also the cloud service providers have already made some popular LMSs ready to be ordered. These LMSs are well migrated and fully hosted over cloud infrastructure and in large-scale and fine-grained. Therefore, the education providers, no matter in different levels or with different requirements, are able to customize the whole or solely part of cloud-hosting LMSs' functions on demand, where exhaustive remaking and resetting are not needed anymore. It is notable that the authorities to access the cloud-hosting LMSs are by renting charged by the usages, which are much cheaper than purchasing their licenses. The reusing of legacy LMSs is feasible due to the data migration technology, which avoids the waste of repetitive deployments for the same kind of LMS in different areas (Gao and Zhai, 2010).

Teachers and administers need neither to be trained like technicians in order to maintain the daily running of LMS, nor to keep abreast of the emerging m-learning technologies. Benefiting from the mobile cloud-based learning, they can pay their full attention to the organization and delivery of the educational content to make learners more interested and knowledge assimilated better (Rao, 2010). This is because the professional teams from the cloud service provider take responsibility for all the technical problems.

Given the cloud can be seen as a huge information pool, the learning resources from all over the world are integrated and shared to maximize the value of knowledge. Through easily querying, such as the key term searching, learners are able to discover and obtain the learning resources then freely choose which are needful to learn. Based on learners' feedbacks and requirements, the update, modification and supplement of learning resources proceed, so as the sole duty of the teachers and administers is to categorise and manage the learning resources and set corresponding access rules.

The mobile cloud-based learning catalyses the emergence of diversified virtual learning communities and virtual teams, which are dismissed the restraint of location, national and culture background of learners and expanded the influence scopes (Liao and Wang, 2011). Therein, learners are free to participate in those kinds of personnel structure of learner cohorts to exchange and discuss their ideas, share their experiences and learn from others' strengths to find and improve their weaknesses. Hence, more collaborative learning has a favourable environment to be happened among learners who have similar learning purposes, so as teamwork is a more and more frequent learning activity and important learning approach in the mobile cloud-based learning (Chua and Tay, 2012).

2.1.4. *Micro Learning*

Research conducted by Yahoo (Gutierrez, 2014) stated that, although users seem to be addicted by mobile devices without willingness to put down their devices, it is not opposite to that they just want to receive and process information rapidly and quickly. Results of a study (Chen & Lin, 2016) revealed that when proceeding m-learning young learners frequently pause their learning activities and transfer their attention to another thing, and commonly the time lasting for their attentions limited in 15 minutes.

Stockwell (2008) analysed the time lasting for young learners' attention in m-learning, the results showed that when proceeding m-learning, their learning activities are frequently interrupted by other activities, so that their attention spans are often limited in 15 minutes.

Micro learning can have positive effects on mastery learning and be an important part of blended learning (Milligan et al. 2013; Zhang & Ren 2011). It can help learners make use of every fragmented piece of time to participate in learning activities in very short terms. Compared to accomplishing a course chunk with one or more interruptions, this can lead to positive effects for them to acquire targeted knowledge (Bruck 2008). Learning in small steps (contrary to the traditional approach of learning through hours-long courses) is made possible with the aid of small and well-planned chunks of units or activities. Thus, micro learning becomes short-term, digestible, and easily manageable (Kovachev et al., 2011). Micro learning also adapts to the constraints of the human brain with respect to its attention span. It is consistent with research finding that proves people learn better when engaged in short, focused sessions, than hour-long sessions that cause information overload (Bruck et al., 2012).

In literature, "micro learning" processes cover a time span from a few seconds (e.g. in mobile learning) to up to 15 minutes or more. Another explanation of micro learning is suggested as: 'micro learning refers to short-term learning activities on small learning units. In the contemporary mobile/web society, micro learning pertains to small pieces of knowledge based on web resources' (Kovachev et al., 2011). Compared to the traditional hours-long e-learning, micro learning features high flexibility, and it can be delivered in various forms, and, more importantly, it has less time limitation. In other words, it can be started anytime, whereas it may also be terminated at anytime.

In mobile learning, learning activities can be conducted in learners' conveniences, regardless the location and time. By this means, learners can get access to learning resources within various scenarios. With mobile devices, quite often learners accomplish learning missions in a short time period. According to the study conducted by Hug and Lindner

(2005), micro learning can be an assumption about the time needed to complete a relevant learning task, for example answering a question, memorizing an information item, or finding learning materials. Hence, micro learning booms with the wide use of mobile devices, and it becomes a major learning means in mobile environment. Micro learning shares some similar specialties with mobile learning as both of them are individually referable, self-contained, reusable and re-mixable (Sanchez-Alonso et al., 2006; Leene, 2006).

Australian educators use different kinds of multimedia to make course more comprehensive, which helps learners understand more effectively. The contents of courses can be reused among different courses. On the other hand, these widely used course materials are in the form of visual information, while educational micro content is suggested to be in the similar form, which may consist of text, video, audio, picture, graph, or drawing, etc. (Liao & Zhu, 2012). Mobile learning and micro learning go hand in hand. People are using their mobile devices more and more in the workplace, for communication as well as for searching answers to questions. It brings learning to employees while they are performing their daily activities, rather than requiring them to leave their work environments (Semingson et al., 2015). Micro learning resources can be made available on-demand to facilitate just-in-time learning (Gassler et al., 2004). These small learning bytes not only aid quick assimilation but also make it possible to learn on the go, thus reducing the dependency on a fixed time slot or the need to take a large chunk of time out of one's working day (Gutierrez, 2014; Anderson et al., 2014).

As micro learning evolves, micro-content delivery with a sequence of micro interactions enables users to learn without information overload (Souza & Amaral, 2014). It is a key technology to ensure better learning outcome in terms of retention of propositional content (Kovachev et al., 2011).

2.2 Open Learning and Open Educational Resources

Open learning, which aims to integrate e-learning and open courses with other learning modes, is vigorously pursued by many education providers. It has been adopted by many regional universities or universities with multiple campus operations (Hilton, 2016). It is quite different from on-campus, e/m-learning mode. This term has been defined by many researchers as early as in the year of 1975, and it keeps evolving all the way. Open learning has resided in public domain and been organized under licenses for free use and any other reuse and repurposing (Harley, 2008).

Open learning seeks to remove all unnecessary barriers to learning, while aiming to provide students with a reasonable chance of success in an education and training system centred on their specific needs and located in multiple arenas of learning (Neil Butcher, 2011). It incorporates several key principles:

- Learning opportunity should be lifelong and should encompass both education and training (Leone, 2018);
- The learning process should be centred on the learners, build on their experience and encourage independent and critical thinking (Hannafin et al., 2013);
- Learning provision should be flexible so that learners can increasingly choose, where, when, what and how they learn, as well as the pace at which they will learn;
- Prior learning, prior experience and demonstrated competencies should be recognized so that learners are not unnecessarily restricted from educational opportunities by lack of appropriate qualifications;
- Learners should be able to load progress or accumulate credits from different learning contexts;
- Providers should create the conditions for a fair chance of learner success.

Resources used in open learning are ranging from full courses, course materials, modules, textbooks, streaming videos, tests, software, and any other tools, materials, or techniques used to support access to knowledge (Atkins et al., 2007). Formally, OERs are 'digital learning resources offered online freely and openly to teachers, educators, students, and independent learners in order to be used, shared, combined, adapted, and expanded in teaching, learning and research' (Hilton, 2016). Researchers summarized the development of OER conforms with a '5R', wherein, the 'Retain' refers to 'make and own copies', the 'Reuse' indicates 'use in a wide range of ways', 'Revise' represents the action of 'adapt, modify and improve', 'Remix' equals to 'combine two or more' and 'share with others' is highlighted by 'Redistribute' (Theeraroungchaisri, 2016).

The following issues mainly account for the speedy development and wide acceptance of the open learning, or, in other words, the utilization of OER.

- Cost: the problem of cost (e.g. for textbooks) comes always at the first place to the user/customer side in the e/m-learning even traditional on-campus learning, where these customers can be either the learners or the education providers. This problem is exposed more significant in developing counties (Lesko, 2013).

- License: Copyright restrictions on textbooks, journals, and other educational objects prevent educators from combining materials in a way that best meets the demands of their students. It also reduces the feasibility to break and re-construct learning resources from different institutions.

- Local Support: Although OER is fully international; there were needs for local support. Chae and Jenkins (2015) summarized from their participants' opinion that they are delighted to have a local OER service unit on campus and a readily available person who are well versed in finding, utilizing, designing and tailoring of OER. These go-to persons help incoming instructional designers, instructors and other stakeholders in open learning to get familiar with the similar operations on OERs, so that they promote the use of OER in both learning and teaching.

2.2.1. *Classification and Evolution of OER (OER, OCW and MOOC)*

a) Open Course Ware

The formal definition for the Open Course Ware (OCW) given by the OCW Consortium organization is "free and open digital publication of university-level educational materials. These materials are organized as courses, and often include course planning materials and evaluation tools as well as thematic content" (OCW Consortium.org). Taking the MIT's

OCW program as example, this pioneer started as early as in 2001. This trend has been extended widely in Europe and Asia.

Generally OCW is a subset of OER (Friesen, 2009). Unlike OER including any educational content that is shared under an open license, whether or not it is a part of a course, OCW sorely focuses on sharing open content that is developed specifically for a course.

b) Massive Open Online Course

Rising remarkably in the recent decade, the Massive Open Online Course (MOOC) is offered free to students of any age group and also works on an open network learning model, with neither formal entry requirement nor participation restrictions. It soon becomes the most eye-catching trend in OER and gains its popularity in the whole higher education sector (King et al., 2014). The explosive growth of learning resources online leads to a revolution of education and learning, and the year of 2012 was named as 'the year of MOOC' (Pappano, 2012).

It is an online course targeting on large-scale interactive participation and open access via the Web, which is an important supplement to the traditional distance education (Liyanagunawardena et al., 2013). It contains interaction, feedback and assessment (via automated quizzes or peers) and even many world-famous universities, who contribute courses to MOOC providers, are gradually accrediting the credits gained from MOOC courses. Therefore, statistics show that millions of people are participating in the virtual classroom of MOOC, particularly; the number of students who are enrolled in a single course at the same time could be as high as tens of thousands (Baggaley, 2013)

Fauvel and Yu (2016) stated following offerings for platforms or courses to be called MOOCs:

- Massive: they should accommodate thousands to tens of thousands of students taking the same course simultaneously;
- Open: they should be freely accessible – anyone can register with no financial barriers, and there are no preconditions for learners;
- Online: they can be accessed through a computing device (e.g. a computer, smartphone or tablet) with an Internet connection;
- Course: they should offer a well-organized learning sequence, but not unconnected learning objects or modules.

MOOCs are generally divided into two broad categories: cMOOCs, which are based on the connectivist pedagogy approach, and xMOOCs, which are similar to traditional university courses (Saadatdoost et al. 2015). cMOOCs focus on the creation of connections between learners, and the course contents are usually not predefined; instead, they move on according to the discussions between learners. xMOOC on the other hand, usually have predefined course contents; learning materials are prepared before start date by instructor(s), and students go through them in the sequence. Today, most of available MOOCs are of the xMOOCs type, whose course contents are uploaded before the start of those online courses (Daniels et al., 2015).

MOOC courses are offered to learners through online platforms, such as Coursera, edX and Udacity. Also, there are hundreds of other available platforms, each of which is with its particular focus, characteristics and features. These platforms generally include the following three components: course contents, community building tools, and platform tools (Fauvel and Yu, 2016). The contents of these components are shown in Figure 2.1.

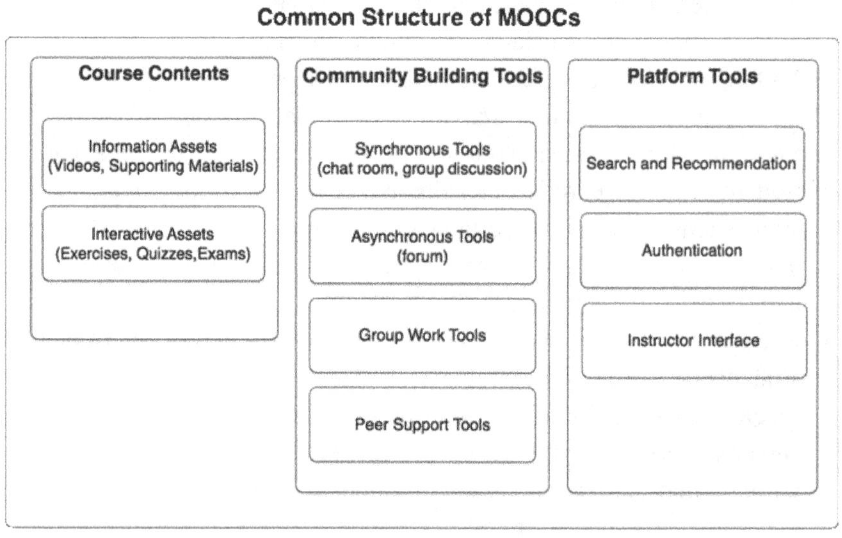

Common Structure of MOOCs

Course Contents	Community Building Tools	Platform Tools
Information Assets (Videos, Supporting Materials)	Synchronous Tools (chat room, group discussion)	Search and Recommendation
Interactive Assets (Exercises, Quizzes, Exams)	Asynchronous Tools (forum)	Authentication
	Group Work Tools	Instructor Interface
	Peer Support Tools	

Figure 2.1: Common Structure of MOOCs Platform

Course contents can be divided into informational assets and interactive assets. Informational assets can be videos (with transcripts), which are the main content delivery strategy in current MOOCs, or other supporting materials such as e-textbooks, lecture slides, lecture notes, topic outline, etc. Interactive assets refer to assessment units such as exercises, quizzes and exams for students to complete. Usually, interactive assets of a course can only be seen by enrolled students.

Community building tools include asynchronous tools, which are not used simultaneously by learners and instructors, such as forums; as well as synchronous tools, which allow learners to share their space simultaneously, such as chat rooms and real-time group discussions. Different platforms are using different tools.

Platform tools usually have searching and recommendation features, as well as user authentication features. Most platforms also provide an interface for teachers to organize their course contents, and some statistics and data visualization tools to support them in teaching.

c) Open Educational Practice

Open educational practice (OEP) is recognized as an important activity in the open learning. Its importance was stated by Armellini and Nie as that "systematic support and training for academics, focusing on evidence and added value for students and themselves" (2013). It expands the scale of open learning from purely one-way knowledge impaction to two-way interactions and hands-on experience. Conole and Ehlers (2010) believed that OEP is able to shift the way instructors pass on knowledge and students obtain information, as they stated that "the use of open educational resources with the aim to improve quality of educational processes and innovate educational environments".

2.2.2. *Instructional Design of OER*

Participants in research by Harley (2008), Lane and McAndrew (2010) and Rolfe (2012) listed a lack of support in terms of training in how to find and use OER as a barrier to the integration of open materials, while Lynch and Rather (2015) noticed there was a lack of institutional support for innovative teaching strategies and practices which can keep in pace with the edge-cutting learning technology. Finding, adapting, and adopting such resources can be complicated by the fact that instructors may lack the knowledge of and/or comfort with using the technologies necessary to conduct needed or desired tailoring. This can limit OER being utilized to its fullest potential. (Armellini and Nie, 2013; Petrides et al., 2011)

The training for instructors and instructional designer in open learning comes up with a new topic to the OER providers. Generally it is closely related to the following concerns (Armellini & Nie, 2013):

- How to find appropriate locations for OER
- How to conduct research around the use of OER;
- How to use the technology needed to find, adapt and adopt OER;
- How copyright works including the types and role of open licences;
- How to create OER using appropriate formats and licenses.

Researchers believed that the over-rapid release of OERs may negatively influent the quality of resource (Davis et al., 2014), as participant OER providers are eager to occupy or keep a place in the highly competitive market (Cormier and Siemens, 2010). It is suggested that solid instructional design can ensure the quality of OERS (Nunez et al., 2014). To kick start a good instructional design, there are five fundamental principles underpin all contemporary models and theories (Merrill, 2002; Merrill, 2013; Collins, 2005; Nunez et al., 2017). They believed learning is promoted when: 1) learners acquire skills in the context of real-world problems; 2) learners activate existing knowledge and skills as a foundation for new skills; 3) learners observe a demonstration of the skill to be learned; 4) learners apply their newly acquired skill to solve problems; 5) learners reflect on, discuss, and defend their newly acquired skill. These fundamental principles have been extended by Margaryan (2008) to conform with the changes in modern education so that learning is further promoted when: 6) learners contribute to the collective knowledge; 7) learners collaborate with others; 8) different learners are provided with different avenues of learning which are according to their needs; 9) learning resources are drawn from real-world settings; 10) learners are given expert feedback on their performance. Corresponding to the sequences they were listed, these principles can be summarized as follows:

(1) Problem-centred: The instructional effectiveness of a course will be enhanced if students solve real-world problems and if the task is divided into smaller ones of increasing complexity.

(2) Activation: The instructional effectiveness of a course will be higher if its activities help students to link previously developed skills to its new knowledge. If those previous skills have not been developed, the course should begin by helping students acquire them.

(3) Demonstration: When learners observe a demonstration of the skill to be learned, learning is promoted. The instructional effectiveness of a course will improve if examples of both poor and good practices are shown, and students are trained to differentiate between them.

(4) Application: Instructional effectiveness will grow if students apply their knowledge in practical exercises, complementing the theoretical exams.

(5) Integration: Instructional effectiveness will improve if students are able to integrate their knowledge into their daily lives and can demonstrate it to others.

(6) Collective Knowledge: Inclusion of forums and other tools where students can exchange opinions, questions, and answers about the learning topic will improve instructional effectiveness.

(7) Collaboration: Activities where students can work with others, and even perform peer-to-peer assessment, will increase instructional effectiveness.

(8) Differentiation: Varied resources with different levels of complexity help customize the learning to individual students and thus enhance instructional effectiveness.

(9) Authentic: Resources previously used in real projects, even if developed by professors, are highly recommended for sharing with students in order to increase instructional effectiveness.

(10) Feedback: Comments on mistakes and opportunities for improvement should be offered to students after their assessments to boost instructional effectiveness.

2.2.3. Benefits of OER

Open learning has the advantage of both informal learning and formal learning. Learners enjoy high flexibilities of online open learning because there is no strict time constraint for joining and quitting. Learners engaged in open learning are in different age groups and from various culture backgrounds, which are with a wide range of geographic distribution. Open learning also can bring learning opportunities to disadvantaged and excluded groups of learners for whom the accessibility of resources was previously unavailable.

The cost-efficiency of OER is considerable and the adoption of OER is fully able to lower the cost for learners. It also has strengths in reducing duplication and promoting inter-institutional cooperation, co-creation and resource sharing, therefore saving time and effort for content development (Windle et al., 2010). Sharing development costs among institutions or OER providers becomes possible. This can also empower collaboration and creativity in OER production.

The adoption of OER increases efficiency and quality of learning resources: teachers have easier access to high-quality learning resources; collaboration and sharing has the potential to further enhance the quality of learning resources and to foster pedagogical innovation due to exposure to large communities of learners and educator.

A recent study found that OER contributes to the local and global community (Godwin-Jones, 2014). Perryman et al. (2014) and Wolfenden et al. (2012) noted that the ability to adapt OER allows for not only adding or removing chapters based on the wishes of the instructor, but to make changes to the text to fit local culture and language better.

2.2.4. OER as a Service (Service-oriented OER Delivery)

There are still some barriers for course instructors to migrate their previous teaching strategies to this new blended learning environment. Owing to the advantages of services oriented and mobile cloud-based learning and more and more popular mobile apps, delivering OER in a service-oriented mode has substantial potentials to be employed by OER providers. For example, as a trial case, OER as a Service, is not only believed to have potential in OER distribution, but also eases the process of service deployment and delivery (Corbi &Burgos, 2016; Hernandez et al., 2014). Service-oriented OER provision encloses the content service, technical service and customer service in a one-stop experience, by using cloud based tools, such as virtual containers (Corbi & Burgos 2016).

2.3 Micro Open Learning

2.3.1. *M-learning in Open Learning*

Without a doubt, mobile learning is getting extensive acceptance by learners and gradually becoming a major learning means (Kim et al., 2006; Sun & Shen, 2014). The benefits of m-learning are well studied in numerous researches. As a result, most MOOC providers promptly released their mobile apps on mainstream mobile operation system (i.e. iOS, Android and WP8) and adapted their webpages to adapt the screen size and operation mode of mobile devices in order to catch the trend of m-learning and enable more convenient use for learners.

OER providers try to popularize their courses and affiliated educational productions at full stretch. They are spreading out their available learning resources everywhere all around the world and they are leveraging m-learning to enable learners to easily participate in learning activities regardless the restriction of time and location. In addition, Mobile cloud-based learning allows learners to participate in open learning or open courses with mobile devices. Learners now have flexible options to access 'big' learning resources, whenever they want, wherever they are (Wang et al., 2014). However, they are still and often at loss. More specifically, although these courses can have a large number of learners enrolled at the very beginning, it is found that they gradually quit halfway. Researchers intend to look for the reasons why OER cannot fascinate learners throughout the overall process of course learning over OER and what elements make the journey feel long and tedious.

As a key concern, the typical product of OER, namely MOOC, is currently suffering from low completion rate, with several sources indicating that about 5% to 15% of participants finish the courses on average while most learners who enrolled in MOOC courses ended up dropping out (Nawrot & Doucet, 2014). However, some authors suggest that dropout statistics might not be representing the only reality of MOOC learners. This is because different patterns of student behaviour exist, and analysing further each participant's objectives can provide additional insight into the different personal goals when attending a course besides finalizing it. Therefore, different measures should be available in order to evaluate whether MOOCs are effective for individual participants (Daradoumins et al., 2013). Arguably, this is mainly because learners fail to conduct effective time management, so that they are suffering from time consuming and conflicts with their real-life responsibilities (Nawrot & Doucet, 2014).

Another crucial factor is believed that, although efforts have been put in, learners deem it is not easy to find appropriate resources they want, or the chosen resources do not match their expectation. In Chae and Jenkin's study (2015), their participants claimed the chance to find and modify materials in a time manner is very insufficient. This viewpoint is also supported by Armellini and Nie's survey finding (2013). They claimed that finding resources across multiple repositories is time-consuming, and that, adapting the resources they have found to meet their individual demands may even take significant longer time than this. Harley, et al. (2010) found that this time commitment was a key reason that learner cannot enjoy their open learning journey. In this case, they simply give up and look for substitutes, and some of them repeatedly enrol to try a new course until they eventually find their preferred ones (Khalil & Ebner 2014).

The third reason is that the backgrounds of learners engaged in MOOC courses are more diversified (DeBoer et al., 2013). Some MOOC learners do not have a concrete aim to complete an entire course as to get the credits, because they only want to acquire the specific knowledge they actually need. Such knowledge is often enclosed in small course units or passed on during phases going by midway of the course delivery. Therefore, once they are satisfied with the progress they have made, they are possible to quit while leaving assignments or tests unfinished (Daradoumins et al., 2013; Khalil & Ebner, 2014).

This can explain why m-learning in MOOC appears distinct from its traditional form and mode in on-campus and distance education. MOOC teaching and learning highly rely on the connectivism approach. Teamwork, collaboration, communication and peer-to-peer learning are of attached important educational value in MOOC. However, despite the advantages of mobile cloud-based learning and forthcoming mobile apps, learning resources for non-mobile devices cannot be directly adapted to mobile device due to their indeterminacies of context, such as unpredictable network bandwidth, and specificities, such as different operation systems. Learners may be at their wits end to choose which courses to learn at first or next when there are many options to be considered. In addition, enhancing learners' teamwork performance in collaborative learning plays a significant role when MOOC learners are achieving their learning objectives as a group. How to enhance learners' teamwork performance comes down to a variety of pedagogical concepts and is scarcely supported by any Web based tools. Hence, some researchers are very concerned that open online courses may not reach its promise because many aspects of traditional classes, such as small-group discussions and face-to-face time with instructors, would not be realized in the MOOC format (Daradoumins et al., 2013). Moreover, it is found that learning activities are off and on frequently during the progress of MOOC course and many learning activities are completed within fragmented pieces of time. In other words, their learning processes become fragmented or of micro size.

2.3.2. *Micro learning over OERs*

Standard models of m-learning, as instructor-led or computer-based, look very much alike college classes, where learners are taken out of their normal work or living environments to spend many hours "learning" activities which they may or may not encounter in their day-to-day lives. However, standard models are quickly being swept out the door by the learning methods that do take place inside the normal work environment, but right smack in the middle of it. This has resulted in new interests in micro learning, which is essentially any type of learning carried out in very short bursts of period. Digital learning environments, like MOOCs, can actually provide frame-works for a wide variety of micro learning activities.

By analysing 6.9 million records of video playing, the industry-leading OER provider edX[c] found that the videos with a time length less than 6 minutes are more attractive, while students' engagements drop sharply after 6 minutes (Guo et al., 2014; Anderson et al., 2014). Regardless the exact length of the videos, the actual median value of viewing time is 6 minutes. In addition, 6-9 minutes videos are in the inflexion, while longer videos have less median values of viewing time.

Hence, according to existing studies to investigate MOOC's learner behaviour tracks, it is not surprising that, to some extent, MOOC follows the principles of micro learning and even MOOC is typically designed around the principles of micro learning, which enables learners to go through bytes of learning in short duration (Guo et al., 2014; Anderson et al., 2014). For instance, some course materials have been chunked and sequenced in a simple-to-complex order to enable faster processing by students. The units ideally do not exceed 15 minutes. For example, one popular way to link two micro course units is to add a simple assessment, normally in the form of quiz, true/false questions or multiple choices, between them (Adamopoulos, 2013).

On the other hand, as stated in the previous Section 2.2, OER learning emphasizes collaboration and connectivism (Makness et al., 2013; Waard et al., 2012), where learner-generated contents are also of importance in OER delivery. It is believed that micro learning is an efficient way to carry out problem-based learning and exchange just-in-time feedback. OER also provides essential basis for life-long learning. The learn-as-you-go mode of micro learning makes people feel free to acquire any particular knowledge they need or are interested in as soon as they want (Kovachev et al., 2011). If they do not have a necessary demand to get credits from OER providers, by micro learning they can still easily get through specific learning content without finishing the entire course. By this means, micro learning can lead to better integration across disciplines in OER provision.

---

[c] https://www.edx.org/course

2.4 Adaptive Learning: Learner Modelling and EDM & LA

2.4.1. *Learner Modelling*

Learner model is a key element of personalized learning systems (Conejo et al. 2011). It usually includes a set of structured information which describes the characteristics of learners (Al-Hmouz et al., 2012). In order to provide personalized learning experience to each individual learner, a way to represent learners and the course materials should be identified first, so that systems can recommend courses which can better fit a learner's interest and current knowledge level.

a) Definition of Learner Model

A learner model is the representation of learner's skills and abilities in computer systems and it enables learning system to adapt to special needs of the learner. A learner model commonly contains a learner's important information, such as: domain knowledge, learning performance, interests, preference, goal, tasks, background, personal traits (e.g. learning style and aptitude), environment and other useful features. According to Kay et al. (1997), the learner model (also known as student model) is defined as "machine's representation of its beliefs about the learner".

A learner model can contain two categories of information, domain specific information or domain independent information (Brusilovskiy, 1994). Domain specific information reveals the status or degree of knowledge and skills that learner obtained in certain knowledge domain. Domain specific information allows adaptive e-learning systems to organize a content related learner model, eliminate what learner already knows, and focus instruction or assessment on areas that the learner is weak at. Domain independent information represents information besides knowledge, such as learning goals, interests, learning styles and personal traits. Domain independent information is related to the learner profile data (e.g. learning style or personality) and it allows the system to serve optimal learning content sequences or presenting formats.

b) Modelling Learner's Knowledge

Domain specific information of a learner is organized as a knowledge model, which contains elements that the learner needs to learn (e.g. concepts, topic, and subject). Generally there are three different forms to model learners' knowledge, namely, vector model, overlay model, and fault model (Nguyen & Do 2008).

- **Vector model:** The vector model represents learner's knowledge in a knowledge domain as a vector, whose elements can be concepts, topics or subjects. Although vector model is the simplest one of the three models, it is very efficient.

- **Overlay model:** The overlay model is one of the most popular and commonly used student models. The underlying assumption of the overlay model is that a learner can have incomplete but correct knowledge of certain knowledge domain (Chrysafiadi & Virvou, 2013). In the overlay model, learners' knowledge is a subset of the domain knowledge, which is represented by an expert's knowledge level of that domain. The differences between learner's knowledge and domain knowledge are assumed to be the learner's lack of knowledge, and the objective of learning is to eliminate these differences as much as possible (Bontcheva & Wilks, 2005). Similar to the vector model, each element in the overlay model is a number, which presents learner's knowledge level against a certain topics or subjects.

- **Fault model:** The drawback of vector model and overlay model is that it cannot describe the misconception of learners over certain knowledge. Fault model can represent learner's errors or misconceptions and the reasons why the learner has these errors (Baschera & Gross, 2010). From fault model, an adaptive learning system can infer what learning materials should be delivered to help learners learn new knowledge as well as eliminate misconceptions.

The data used for modelling learner's knowledge usually comes from two different sources, by assessments (e.g., pre-tests before taking a course, quizzes during course, or exams) or surveys (Shute & Towle, 2003). In the study conducted by Pardos et al. (2013), learner's knowledge is estimated using discrete knowledge components defined by a domain expert. Each assessed problem was a knowledge component, which was then be modelled by a Bayesian Knowledge Tracing based method. With this model, researchers can predict whether a learner has successfully acquired a certain knowledge component during their course. This approach requires expert to input domain specific knowledge components. Yudelson et al. (2014) used a variant of Additive Factors Model to automatically extract the domain model by exploiting the structure of Java programming language and then model student knowledge. Compared to the previous method, this approach is completely automated, yet it is only applicable within the programming domain. Also, learners' knowledge can be estimated using a specific assessment tool both before and after the course (Konstan et al., 2015). To identify factors that can predict how much knowledge the learners gained, an Ordinary Least Squares (OLS) regression model was built, from which they found that all predictive factors are relevant to efforts that the learners have put into the course (as measured by the number of activities), prior courses taken, and baseline knowledge.

In above approaches, learner models are usually hidden from learners, where learners do not have access to learner models. While in recent years, there is a growing trend to make learner models open. The Open Learner Model presented by Bull and Kay (2010) is a well-known example of this approach. Open learner models refer to learner models that can be browsed or modified in some way by learners themselves or by other users (e.g. teachers, peers, parents). Therefore, besides the purpose of enabling adaptive learning according to learner's current needs, the learner can also directly use the contents of learner model. Making learner models open brings following potential benefits (Bull & Kay, 2007).

- Promoting metacognitive activities such as reflection, planning and self-monitoring;
- Allowing the learners to take greater control and responsibility over their learning, and encouraging their independence;
- Facilitating navigation to materials, exercises, problems or tasks;
- Supporting assessment of learner's knowledge gain;
- Increasing the accuracy of learner model data.

If having access to the information in learner model has the potential to benefit the user, the learner model built with any learner modelling technique could be opened to the learner. For instance, learner models were opened in simple weighted numerical models (Bull & Gardner, 2009), fuzzy models (Mohanarajah et al., 2005), and Bayesian models (Zapata-Rivera & Greer, 2004).

2.4.2. *EDM and LA*

Student learning data collected by open learning systems are explored to develop predictive models by applying educational data mining methods that classify data or identify relationships. These models play a key role in building adaptive learning systems, in which adaptations or interventions based on the model's predictions can be used to change what students experience next, or even to recommend academic services to support their learning.

At this cutting edge, EDM and LA are widely used in research. They are used to build models in several areas that can influence online learning systems. As its name implies, EDM is a state of the art method that applies data mining techniques to educational data. It is concerned with many developing methods, and acts on exploring the unique types of data in educational settings. Using these methods, students and educational settings can be better understood (Romero et al., 2010). To enable smart and adaptive micro learning for MOOC, EDM and LA are key concepts that we employ to build the basis of the dynamic learner model construction.

Generally, OCW data is locked away in independent data silos hosted by different OCW/OER providers. This makes it much less useful than it could be. It is difficult to develop tools for consuming data from multiple silos. Searching OCW/OER across multiple silos means invoking the user interface of each one, and receiving the results in separate groups. The presence of data silos makes accessing data and interoperability between repositories harder in several ways.

Browsing OERs also has a problem as each silo has its own organizational structure. Some silos cannot be linked to a particular item, which hinders the free flow of information. The presence of OCW silos impedes the interoperability, discovery, synthesis, and flow of knowledge. As a result, it is a difficulty for teachers, students and self-learners to look for resources, and sometimes they make decisions based on incomplete information. Linked data have the potential to create bridges between OCW data silos (Nelson et al., 2014).

2.4.3. *Big Data in Education*

Analysing these newly logged events requires new techniques for working with unstructured text and image data, data from multiple sources, and vast amounts of data ("big data"). Big data does not have a fixed size; any number assigned to define it would change as computing technology advances to handle more data. For example, Manyika et al. defined big data as "datasets whose size is beyond the ability of typical database software tools to capture, store, manage, and analyse." (Manyika et al., 2001).

The emerging 'big data' concept values the systematic and real-time data, which was difficult to track and store due to technical limitations. Therefore, underlying patterns are feasible to be discovered in order to predict student outcomes, such as dropping out, requirements for extra assistance, or desires for higher demanding assignments or course settings (Picciano, 2012). By this means, learning resources can be predictive and diagnostic. In other words, how learners will perform on the learning process can be evaluated and instructional techniques can be further employed to tailor learning for individual learner's particular needs.

Armed with statistical information compiled from various digital systems, numerous dashboards software and data warehouses have been developed with this big data trend. Benefitting from this, education providers are allowed to monitor learning, performance and behavioural issues, for individual learners as well as for the institute as a whole. Data visualization technique enables key metrics to be collated in a simple-to- and easy-to-interpret interface (Williamson, 2016). Therefore, how the learning is proceeding as well as how the organization is hosting are quickly and directly reflected on such dashboards, where data from various streams are translated to present clear and comprehensive overviews.

The leveraging of big data lifts the EDM and LA to a more effective and efficient extent, whose growth is certified to reshape the way in which the forthcoming generation will learn (Sin & Muthu, 2015).

Summary

In this chapter we have reviewed the literatures that are relevant to our research. In the Section 2.1, the background of mobile learning and micro learning was discussed along with the development of distance learning. The features and benefit as well as instructional design issues of OER and open learning were summarized in the Section 2.2. Motivated by the advantages of these two new learning trends, we explored the feasibility to make use of the micro open learning for the sake of offering better learning contexts and experiences in the Section 2.3. Common approaches adopted in the implementation of adaptive learning, for example, learner modelling and EDM and LA, were discussed together with the effects brought by the rising big data concept, which can be found in the Section 2.4.

Chapter 3

Research Design

The explosive growth of learning resources online, especially the massive open online course (MOOC) leads to a revolution of education and learning (Baggaley, 2013). Educational professionals have strived extraordinarily on exploring the OER format as a regular pedagogical approach for mobile learning (m-learning) (Waard et al., 2011). However, as research and development of OER are still in its infancy, there are evidently many opportunities to improve the learning mechanisms in OER, such as more effective learning platforms and learning support services, to enable easier access and better experience for both service providers and learners.

In our pilot study, we investigated the development trend and acceptance of OER, particularly in Australia, and analysed existing shortcomings as well as its potential improvement directions. Motivated by the observations from this investigation, we designed a mobile service-oriented system which targets on organizing a personalized learning environment (PLE) to support smart collaborative and micro open. In addition, we particularly concentrate on providing a better context and environment for both OER providers and learners to smartly deliver learners adaptive learning resources in small chunks, which are supposed to be learnt in relatively short time duration, and sequencing these courses chunks in series as an identified learning path. Therefore, learners will be able to make the best use of the fragmented pieces of time so as to effectively engage in the micro open learning.

The rest of this chapter will introduce the design of our research, which will be organized as follows: it will start from the research background, where a personalized learning environment (PLE) built in our previous work will be briefly demonstrated; the pilot study will be involved in the research motivation as expounded in the Section 3.2; the challenges we were facing before we commence this research will be summarized in the Section 3.3; after which the research purpose and research design will be rolled out in the following Section 3.4, where example scenarios of micro OERs adaptation will be also taken for easier understanding; the system framework, which will serve as a basis of this research, can be inspected in the Section 3.5.

3.1 Research Background

Open learning performs quite differently from on-campus e/m-learning mode. OERs are "digital learning resources offered online freely and openly to teachers, educators, students, and independent learners in order to be used, shared, combined, adapted, and expanded in teaching, learning and research." (Hylen et al., 2012). Open learning is the combination of informal learning and formal learning. Learners enjoy high flexibilities in online open learning because there is no strict time constraint for joining and quitting. Learners engaged in open learning are across age groups and culture background with a wide range of geographic distribution.

Generally OERs can be differentiated from MOOC and open courseware (OCW). Contrary to MOOC, OCW only offers course materials rather than entire courses. In other words, OER can be either structured (MOOC content) or unstructured (i.e. OCW), even both of them. OER providers and instructors have tried to promote their courses and affiliated educational products at full stretch. They have leveraged mobile learning (m-learning) for learners to easily participate in learning activities regardless of restrictions in time and location.

From another aspect, mobile learning activities in open learning normally consist of two sections: online learning and offline learning (Trifonova & Ronchetti 2006). Since mobile learners can freely download materials into their mobile devices for viewing offline, they do not often stay with open learning platforms and attend virtual classrooms (Attewell, 2005)). In fact, accessing OERs or any other 'non-open' (or private) learning resource online is only a part of pervasive learning; more tasks associated with pervasive learning would require activities offline (Wu et al. 2010; Lossman & So, 2010), such as data collection, data analysis, and report writing for an assignment. Logically, mobile open learning is through online systems that include guided and instructional materials, the transaction details and deliverable resources (Ally & Samaka, 2013). Hence, while learners are able to accomplish many of their open learning tasks offline, for some necessary procedures, such as data entry and work submission, they need to go back online to conduct these specific tasks.

3.1.1. *Stakeholder Prospective in Adaptive Micro OER*

Typical adaptive learning projects always contain targets and strategies for researchers, application partners and developers (Alario-Hoyos et al., 2014). From the educational institutions' prospective, though being under pressure, they aim to assure openness in their education distribution and enlarge the influence and popularity of it. Aside from teachers/lecturers and learners, the development and application of adaptive OER delivery usually involve educational institute, instructional designers, technicians; and, to a greater content, institutional staff, library staff and system administrators (Alario-Hoyos et al., 2014). They collaborate in the preparation and enactment of the OER delivery and work towards the prosperity of open learning (Khalil & Ebner, 2016).

The leveraging of adaptive micro open learning aims to fulfil learners and educators' needs by incorporating more helpful services into micro open learning and fostering the world-wide development of OER. Meanwhile, it can lead to a better integration of the education resources across institutions to maximize the educational outcomes for a broader spectrum of learners, whether formally enrolled in courses or not.

A timely and feasible solution will be provided for OER providers to offer their services in a smarter manner by matching resources to personalized learning demands. Another outcome of this project will be cost effectiveness, as course providers can combine external resources without any huge re-development of their existing platforms. The novel learning technologies will allow educational organizations and course-instructors to wisely focus on, and tailor their teaching strategies to meet the requirements of, massive learner classes.

3.1.2. *Service-oriented Environment for Mobile OER Delivery*

A key catalyst for m-learning to thrive is the service-oriented and cloud computing paradigms, which harness economic benefits of large scale distributed systems, where computing resources are seamlessly integrated across geographical boundaries. Learners now have numerous options to make decisions for their own to access big learning resources, whenever they want, wherever they are.

In mobile environment, the system needs to provide learners with only the textual or visual learning material, but also software and apps, intuitive and task-oriented user interfaces (UIs), clear and easy-to-follow operation logics, engaging experiences in associated courseware and learning settings. All of these are anticipated to be wrapped up and delivered in a one-stop mode. An ideal way to distribute such OERs is to deliver them as services. This can make the whole process of OER delivery user-transparent, and minimize the hardware requirement for mobile devices.

3.1.3. *Previous Work*

Many educational professionals still evaluate the pros and cons of the OER to foresee whether it can act as a regular, or barely complementary, pedagogical approach for m-learning. Particularly, from the upside, the adoption of OER expands access to learning, enlarges the scalability, lessens the expenses for students, and augments regular course content; from the downside, it suffers from quality issue and does not hold a mature mechanism to deal with the lack of human, especially face to face interactions, between instructors and learners. In addition, because of the new ness of the phenomenal education trend, its popularity has been limited due to the lack of personalized services so that current OER delivery often fails to meet comparatively diverse demands from both OER providers and learners. In other words, it is anticipated to have OER delivered in a personalized learning environment (PLE) rather than a solely traditional virtual learning environment (VLE). Moreover, these OERs are suggested to be consumed in a micro learning mode, which conforms to the characteristic of the modern e-society where mobile and pervasive computing becomes dominant.

Having investigated the feasibilities to improve the resources delivery and learning experiences of MOOC, and the potential benefits of leveraging cloud computing, we are inspired to design a comprehensive cloud-based system, which builds a PLE to have both learners and instructors engaged in through mobile devices. As shown in Figure 3.1, it consists of a couple of Software as a Service (SaaS) and three functional Web services. All services and applications in the PLE will work in conjunction and be deployed over a cloud infrastructure to borrow the strong computing capability and massive storage space so as to offer learners a one-stop interface with transparent, hence easier, operations and lesser software and hardware requirements.

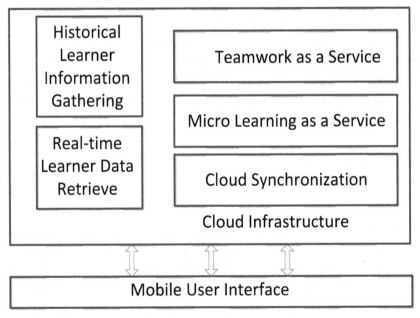

Figure 3.1. Framework of Mobile PLE for MOOC

Combining the features of the mobile cloud environment, where applications are normally interoperable and platform independent, a feasible way to realize the whole teamwork-enhanced learning process is to orchestrate a learning flow, including time sequences, logical relationships, connected patterns and occurring conditions of various learning activities. Learning flow refers to the formal description of a set of rules and the process during which the learning activities occur or change (Cao et al., 2009). A completed learning flow blends all activities together to form a suitable process.

A teamwork-enhanced learning flow is realized by one SaaS, named Teamwork as a Service (TaaS) in the PLE, in order to facilitate collaborative learning. As a part of the whole PLE, TaaS has been developed and implemented over a typical cloud infrastructure, Amazon EC2. Five web services in TaaS can be de-coupled or re-coupled according to specific teaching demands, although it is recommended for them to be utilized as a whole to add a complete set of functions to legacy LMSs. Particularly, as TaaS has its own user interfaces and can work as plug-and-play, it will maintain its own full and independent registration and administration mechanisms.

The details of TaaS has been presented in (Sun & Shen, 2014), including a genetic algorithm enclosed to discover computational choices of grouping strategy (Sun et al. 2013). In this book we will focus on the other SaaS, namely Micro Learning as a Service (MLaaS) which will be introduced in the rest of the Chapter.

3.2 Research Motivation

3.2.1 *Pilot Study*

Online learning through OER is one of the latest technologies in the field of education. OER, as an emerging technology-supported product, is evolving into new pedagogy to benefit both teachers and students. It is offered free to students of any age group and also works on an open network learning model. It enables participants to be connected beyond the traditional learning environment, thereby offering autonomy and openness. As the growing trend of encouraging connected learning among students, it is needed for teachers to participate in an online course. Connected learning indicates that learning can happen outside classroom and through online networks and interactions (Kharbach, 2012). Learning can take place informally by taking part in webinars, attending workshops, listening to Podcasts. This shows very clearly that a 21st century educator has to be well connected, in order to prepare students for their career. It is suggested that educators' participation in open learning would help them encourage their students to effectively use their digital literacy for learning.

The rising of OERs place significant challenges for what is becoming accepted as mainstream practice in learning analytics. As OERs is a widespread yet very new phenomenon, there is not yet a substantial body of literature on the learning analytics of OERs. There is limited analysis of data in OER (Daradoumins et al., 2013). This pilot study intended to identify the features of OER that may influence the Australian educators and to develop a better understanding of how higher education institutions as OER providers can inspire learners in order to increase their performance. We have conducted a survey to collect views regarding OER development and utilization from educators and practitioners in leading Australia education institutions. We were mainly interested in the benefits of OERs for Australian educators, and how we can encourage the Australian educators to use OERs. Using typical statistic methods to analyse their feedback, the main findings can be summarized as follows:

- Educators' intention is to continue using OERs.
- OERs have high importance regarding facilitating the presentation of online learning.
- OERs have low importance regarding providing instructors to learners.
- OERs have low importance regarding facilitating the instructions between collages.
- OERs have high importance regarding reuse of materials.
- OERs have low importance regarding automatic integration of results.
- OERs have low importance regarding free learning options.
- It is very important that within OERs educators do not provide enough support to students.

- It is very important for educators that OERs do not let them have face to face interaction with students.
- It is not very important for educators that within OERs they cannot use perfect course design.
- OERs have high importance regarding mastery learning
- OERs have high importance regarding blended learning.

Details of the pilot study can be referred to (Sun et al. 2015). Among these findings, a noticeable future of OER is mastery learning. In mastery learning, students demonstrate the understanding of a concept through repeated assessment and exposure to material before moving on to the next lesson (Chen et al., 2013). In many traditional classes, if a student attempts a homework assignment and does not do well, he or she simply gets a low score on the assignment and instruction moves to the next topic, providing the student a poor basis for learning the next concept. The feedback is also often given weeks after the concept was taught, by which point students barely remember the material and rarely go back to review the concepts for better understanding. However, in the OER, the technology makes it easy to provide immediate feedback on concepts students do not under-stand. In many cases, Australian educators can provide randomized versions of the same assignment, so that a student can restudy and reattempt the homework. According to Chen et al. (2013), the instructor's tools are designed to facilitate the use of question banks with extensive randomization. This strategy is aligned with general aim to leverage technology to support effective pedagogical approaches.

Another important factor for educators is the ability of blended learning. Blended learning (the strategic combination of face-to-face and online learning experiences) is growing in popularity within higher education and is a new educational model with great potential to increase student outcomes and create exciting new roles for teachers (Poon, 2013). The Centre for the Support and Advancement of Learning and Teaching in a reginal university of Australia, University of the Sunshine

Coast[a], helps academic staff implement blended learning strategies into their courses and programs to enhance the students 'experience and the quality of learning and teaching'. With this modern technology, teachers no longer have to begin from scratch if they have a desire to teach using a blended learning model. With the recent explosion of digital educational resources, it is feasible to examine free resources, research the use of a learning management system and be prepared for potential setbacks in the road on the blended learning path (Chen et al., 2013). These ways can help a teacher dive right into blending learning.

3.2.2 Research Motivation for Adaptive Micro Learning

By investigating current research gaps and challenges, and considering the natural of mastery learning and blended learning of open learning, we are motivated to pro-pose a study to introduce adaptive micro learning into open learning scenarios to tackle the following problems:

- Given learners are using micro learning mode in random and self-regulated manner, we aim to provide them a smart environment to be smartly engaged into open learning via mobile devices, according to their current time availability.
- This study is looking for a solution to provide learners appropriate learning resources from the huge pool where massive courses and affiliated contents are available. This new approach can be used either for learners who wish to complete an entire course to get credits, or those who just acquire the specific knowledge they actually need.
- For the former learners, this study structure knowledge points/course units in series to assemble as entire learning experiences. Specifically, for low completion rate of MOOC, they are able to make the best use of every fragmented time pieces so as to conduct effective time management.
- For the latter learners, who are often quit half-way once they are satisfied with their learning achievement, the proposed approach also

---

[a]   https://www.usc.edu.au/explore/structure/divisions/centre-for-support-and-advancement-of-learning-and-teaching

looks through and compares all course units provided from different education institutions and further places their demands accurately in or across parallel resources. This enables them to gain their task-related knowledge or get skilled training in a short time.

3.2.3 Research Motivation for Online Computation

MLaaS is influenced by the shortage of learner information in the reality of OER deliveries where learners normally join the learning processes in an ad-hoc mode, which hence leads to the difficulty in making a computational decision of micro OER adaptations to learners' real needs. This motivated us to develop a novel solution to tackle the famous cold-start problem, which will be introduced as one of the main contributions of this book (Sun et al., 2017). This solution aims to build an online computation to evidently support the first decision-making process of micro learning adaptation (Sun et al. 2017).

3.3 Research Challenges

3.3.1 Research Challenges in Micro OER Delivery

Some researchers doubt that open online courses and OER delivery may not reach its promises because many aspects of traditional classes, such as small-group discussions and face-to-face interactions with instructors, do not work in the open online format (Franzoni & Assar, 2009). OER makes information available to people at any time, at any place, and in any form, but the key challenge is to not only transmit the right contents at the right time but also actually do it in the right way. OER providers have recognized that current open learning platforms can neither guarantee learners to enjoy their learning experience, nor receive timely feedback of their learning results in an open and connected environment. Several key areas have been recognized as critical for future blended learning applications: new mobile apps, deeper international expansion through translation and geographical partnership distribution, online courses platform to enable third-party apps and integrations, and new features to encourage more collaboration among students (Pinola, 2011).

OER providers try to ensure that the contents are being presented in a univocal manner, whereas the environment is configurable by the instructors; the courses are easily managed; and the exams are standardized. However, the reality remains unsatisfied since online courses lack proper control, verification, or monitoring of these targets (Kukulska-Hulme, 2013).

There are some barriers for course instructors to migrate their previous teaching strategies to this new blended learning environment straightway. Although utilizing mobile cloud-based learning and forthcoming mobile apps bring multiple advantages, learning resources for non-mobile devices cannot be directly adapted to mobile devices because of their indeterminacies of context (e.g. unpredictable network bandwidth), and specificities (e.g. different operation systems).

In some MOOC courses, instructors borrow the principles of micro learning to redesign their courseware and associated settings. Their actions include chunking the course materials and repackaging them in order to make learners easily go through the whole bytes of learning chunks within a short duration which ideally does not exceed the limit of 15 minutes (Kovachev et al., 2011). They prefer to use quizzes or games to link two chunks (Guo et al., 2014). However, these efforts are still in the trial format and have not been applied to larger scale OER production and delivery.

The MOOC is sorely a subset of OERs, which means that the size of OER is even much larger than 'massive'. Meanwhile, OER is flourishing with the era of big data. With the users of MOOC reaching millions, relevant data associated with OERs are fast generated and users are continuously in geometric growth, in regards to the learners, courses, educational institutions, networking, and technical details and so on. When facing massive options as a result of the exponential increase in learning materials available in OERs, learners may be too puzzled to choose the right courses to learn early or late, especially when they only prepare to make short-term effort at once and have to make a decision immediately. Similarly, how to set and select the appropriate objectives and directions, which stand out from the numerous available resources, brings a challenge for both OER providers and instructors.

Micro learning can be used as part of 'push' applications, in which an instructor determines what learning units to deliver when and where, or as 'pull' applications, in which a learner decides when and how to access the learning resources (Guo et al., 2015). However, open learning is mostly in the distance and online manner while learners are in high geographic diversities. Hence, it is difficult for open learning instructors to provide feedback in a timely manner. Instructors' guidelines cannot fit all learners enrolled in the same course as well.

The problem is even more pronounced in m-learning, as devices themselves may cause distractions such as phone calls, email alerts and social network apps (e.g. Facebook, Twitter and WhatsApp etc.). The average mobile user also has a short attention span (Kunznekoff & Titsworth 2012; Chen & Lin, 2016)— most people skim headlines and prefer bite-size content than long articles when surfing over mobile network.

Micro learning with mobile devices requires learners' concentration and reflection. However, Disruptions can come from external environment when learning in movement where unpredictable conditions are more likely to occur. This leaves the mobile learners with a highly fragmented learning experience. To stand this distracted learning experience, learners need to pay more attentions and reflections. Therefore, learning contents should be able to engage with learners instantly, i.e., to give them contents that they are interested in the first place (Sarrab, 2015). Researchers believe that the small screen size of mobile devices restrict information transmission, and the different type of learning content adversely affect the knowledge assimilation performance as well (Chen & Lin, 2016). Hence, avoiding cognitive load is necessary by eliminating any unrelated or decorative materials, which only serve to drive learners' attention away from actual information. Moreover, the most important information needs to be mentioned first or in an obvious place in micro OERs. This can help users absorb the key information even though they are unable to finish a module at a time.

In micro open learning, each learning activity is anticipated to be short but complete, and each OER chunk needs to be available as a stand-alone module (Gassler et al. 2014). In other words, each micro OER must be self-containing and can be used independently. Moreover, proposed micro OERs are able to be aggregated, they can be grouped or re-joined into larger collections of content, or clusters with similar topics (Cakula & Sedleniece, 2013).

Researchers and practitioners are interested in developing artificial intelligence based systems to support adaptive learning (Adamopoulos, 2013). Online learning systems incorporating user data analysis in response to individual student's performance would create adaptive learning environments (Daradoumin et al., 2013). There are a few studies, including our pilot work (Al-Hmouz et al., 2010), exploring the use of smart systems that implement learning resources adaptation. These efforts focus on university level e/m-learning, without looking into the larger open learning scene (Wang, 2008). It is also found that some measures can be effective to realize adaptive learning for an entire course, but are not workable for the fragmented learning activities because of different time schedules of individual learners during the whole course.

Both the providers/instructors and the adaptive open learning systems must play an important role in reaching the goal of maximizing the advantages of OERs. For OER providers/instructors, especially MOOC teachers and course designers, they need to redesign their syllabi, break their entire courses into smaller units and pre-pack them with associated settings. For adaptive open learning systems, the major problem is how to make OERs micro and guide learners to make accurate footsteps sustainably so as to form a footprint that comes with fruitful outcomes. This also being the main gap that we attempt to bridge in our work.

Moreover, there are studies indicating that personality and learning styles play significant roles in influencing academic achievement (Sun and Shen, 2014). As learners commonly do not have sufficient expertise in customizing learning schedules for themselves, and perhaps they are not familiar with their own learning styles, there are high probabilities that they cannot access the right sets of micro content. This may affect them to achieve satisfactory learning outcomes though a lot of time might be spent. In the current situation, learning resources are generally divided and wrapped up by education providers or course lecturers. It considerably lacks flexibilities to fit every specific learner's time availability so that learner should get accommodated to the time length of course setting and manage to squeeze time to accomplish those learning activities.

3.3.2 Research Challenge for Online Computation Problem

Latest recommender systems, which are commonly seen in the e-business, e-entertainment and e-tourism fields, tend to combine offline and online computation together to support the decision-making process of resource recommendation (Gomez-Uribe & Hunt, 2015). This innovation has been rarely found in e-learning and mobile learning (m-learning) platforms and systems, whereas successful cases in e/m-learning generally consume 'big data' when working in close association with the learner historical behaviours. Booming with the rising 'big data' trend and embracing the power of cloud, educational data mining (EDM) and learning analytics (LA) approaches become popularly adopted by well-developed e/m-learning systems in organizing their computing processes, which are commonly offline (Romero & Ventura, 2010). EDM and LA play important roles in substantially increasing the thoroughness of how the computer science and education science can understand the learning participants, scenarios and cases, therefore improving their recommendation quality, in terms of accuracy and personalization. However, these systems normally take 'day' as the finest granularity in their sole offline computation. Their time effectiveness is deficient by failing to keep user information up-to-date, and also the learning re-source adaption process may suffer from the sparsity of data (Souza & Amaral, 2014).

The adoption of online computation part in learning resource recommender systems remains low because unlike online shopping and entertainment, the experience and outcome of micro open learning highly depend on the educational settings, learners' personal learning styles, and, specifically, variable environment and fragmented time frame (Hug & Lindner, 2005). Activities in micro open learning have high randomness, without hard set-ting of beginning and ending. In addition, new OERs, in either micro or non-micro modes, are rapidly released and updated day by day. Fast response mechanisms are needed to insert incoming micro OERs into candidate lists for recommendation.

In addition, in micro open learning, the accumulation and attenuation of user interests and demands can be periodical and may vary in different patterns than other online activities (Romero & Ventura, 2010; Bruck et al., 2012). For example, in e-business, it is meaningless that a product with repetitive function is placed in recommendation list provided that a customer has purchased a similar one not long ago. Also, in e-entertainment and e-tourism, it is less encouraged to recommend the customers products right after they have consumed a similar service not long ago. However, in micro open learning, it is very likely to see that a learner accesses OERs covering similar knowledge are-as again (and again) offered by different educational institutions. This cross-learning phenomenon can be attributed to purposes of reviewing or mutual supplementation, by comparing the ways of knowledge imparting as well as learning two or more micro OERs simultaneously (Nawrot & Doucet, 2014; Miranda et al., 2013).

Both open learning and micro learning are comparatively novel to many people in the e-society. A fresh learner can be at his/her wits end to commence micro open learning given that the available resources are massive, meanwhile, the system faces difficulty to make recommendation because little is known about the learner (Bruck et al., 2012; Lika et al., 2014). This places the cold start problem as the central challenge of micro OER delivery.

3.3.3 *Research Challenge for Cold Start Problem*

In computer science literature, widely used adaptive recommendation methods generally rely on three main categories, i.e., memory-based, model-based and content-based algorithms (Sieg et al., 2010; Liao & Chang, 2016). Although they have been found in many successful cases of recommender systems, for example, the Amazon online store, it is usually difficult to provide reliable recommendations due to the insufficiency of initial data of ratings or preferences. This leads to the occurrence of the well-known cold start problem. Commonly the cold start problem is triggered by three factors: new community, new item and new user.

The cold start problem becomes more severe in the open learning, especially in micro learning through OERs (Bruck, 2012). Both open learning and OER are relatively new products, which have been emerging in the very recent years. Meanwhile, the followers of this novel trend, no matter new education pursuers or regular learners migrated from other online learning modes, newly join into this emerging community of e-society. On the other hand, the learning demands and expectations of learners engaged in open learning are much more practical than conventional university students. In other words, they are mostly self-regulated so that it is totally flexible for them to decide when to join or quit the online course at their own willingness, and switch among courses frequently (Miranda et al., 2013). Consequently, for OER providers, it is difficult to establish a model and update it accordingly for any individual learner because they do not have historical data in hand.

In micro open learning, it is very normal to find that learners take part in and deviate from the learning scenarios frequently, as well as turning on and off the learning activities at their own willingness. In other words, the overall situation of micro learning varies all the way, from individual to individual. Moreover, it is very common that freshmen join into open learning or existing learners unfold a brand-new course learning profile, at any time. All in all, there are a large number of new learners in open learning context; and new learners usually initiate access of new learning re-sources; and existing learners can commence, restart and switch to a new journey of learning very often; and learners who consume learning resources in the same discipline will form as a new community.

If treated inappropriately, the cold start problem may lead to the loss of learners who previously engaged in open learning and then decide to stop using the OER delivery system or adopting this new learning mode (Sun et al., 2016). The reasons behind the situation are mainly due to the lack of accuracy in the recommendations received in that first stage, in which the learners have not yet cast a significant number of votes or ratings to feed the recommender systems. The scarcity of data affects the user satisfaction and then it can further affect the user acceptance of the new open learning mode.

Thus, if a learner is known scarcely by the OER system, the online computation should be able to treat it as a cold-start problem and tackle it by filling in the gaps with predicted data, in order to assist OER providers and instructors to guarantee the quality the first delivery, which can further help to accelerate the ongoing offline computation so as to promote the learner engagement in the upcoming open learning.

3.4 Research Purpose

3.4.1 *Research Purpose*

To address the challenges raised in the Section 3.3, as well as to investigate potential research opportunities in this novel variety of m-learning and open learning, in this research we target on to promote online course learners' personalized learning experiences, and how to make their micro learning more effective and efficient in micro-contexts. The anticipated outcomes of our research are concluded as follows:

- A framework of a smart cloud-based system which aims to provide adaptive micro OERs as well as learning path identifications customized for each individual learner.
- A comprehensive learner model that allows the system to consider individual learning styles, learner's contexts, application capabilities, and teaching materials structure, leading to a customization of the type and delivery format of learning information in response to the user.
- A knowledge base that fills the gap of formal OER structuring, description, and inference.
- A solution for organizing online computation in MLaaS and a heuristic approach for addressing cold start problem in the recommendation of micro OERs.

3.4.2. *Scenario Example of Micro OER Delivery*

In a typical working scenario of our proposed adaptive micro learning framework, the system tailors each course chunk and makes it fit a specific time scale. Supposedly, while learners are conducting open learning using fragmented pieces of time. In this case, learners will be able to use each time piece to go through a chunk completely, neither with any unexpected pause or break-down, nor leaving any unfinished part to next available time.

To better understand the micro OER delivery process, we conclude the contents from the previous sections in this chapter and take the following typical scenarios and the activities involved in each as example:

- *It is 9am at morning and Jack is travelling to work by train. He utilizes the 20-minute journey to improve himself by taking an online course of 'business management' offered by a well-known open learning provider, edX. His mobile phone is empowered by a 4G network. He is in a full carriage, surrounded by passengers who are chatting. MLaaS makes him reviewing a 5-page lecture notes followed by a multiple-choices with 20 questions in regards to the content in the lecture notes.*

- *An undergraduate student Michael, who is enrolled in an Asian university, manages to extend his knowledge regarding the 'business intelligence' for which he takes a subject with the same topic in this semester. He links to a free Wi-Fi provided by a shopping centre and turns on the MLaaS app while he is waiting for a friend. MLaaS direct him to a reading list posted by a leading US university and suggests him a specific article which contains several typical successful cases of business intelligence application.*

- *At a short coffee-break of a session, Roger is trying to make up few points in his presentation content before delivering it. This presentation is about the future trend of eBusiness in Australia and he did a deep research on the topic of 'supply chain management' when he was preparing the presentation in the recent few days. Based on his learning history and progress, the system recommends him a partial section of a lecture video, with a focus on definition and concept of 'supply chain management' and a time length of 9 minutes, from the 'eBusiness' courseware available from an Australia open learning platform.*

- *A retired elder Duncan wants to know more about the Italian history. He picks up his basic smart phone, say iPhone 4, while he is waiting for the ticking from the oven timer. MLaaS delivers him an audio of a brief introduction of 'Renaissance' and several photos of famous paintings and sculptures along with their audio commentary from the museum where they are kept.*

- *A Japanese full-time staff is pursuing a degree of 'electronic engineering' online in the purpose of further promotion in his career. He collects credits from universities involved in Coursera. MLaaS jointly suggests him courses taught in English and Japanese. While he is logging into MLaaS using a tablet, he is introduced into a demo laboratory practice of 'signal processing'.*

From the learners' perspective, by leveraging MLaaS, the most important benefit for them is that they are given sufficient opportunities to make use of fragmented pieces of time to achieve learning outcomes. Also, in the view of usefulness and ease of use of MLaaS, they can have their preferred OERs delivered instantly and accurately, which are expected to operate easily and run smoothly over mobile devices. An ideal micro OER delivered is easy to go through, neither too long to be with any unexpected pause or break-down, nor too short to leave any unfinished part to next available time.

3.5 System Framework

As stated in the Section 3.1.4, a PLE over a cloud has been organized according to the adaptive micro learning requirements, where MLaaS serves as a master service to search and find all available OERs and its associated services, and then it uses online and offline computation components to jointly make the decision of learning resource delivery (Sun et al., 2015; Sun et al., 2017). It aims to deliver learners adaptive micro learning resources in terms of their time availabilities by taking into account the specialties of the micro learning environment as well as the learners' 'highly-mobile' learning behaviours. MLaaS's framework has been well designed in terms of a genuine cloud standard, and its user model has been theoretically constructed by investigating comprehensive pedagogical literature and successful e-learning cases. The architecture of online and offline computation is shown in Fig. 3.2.

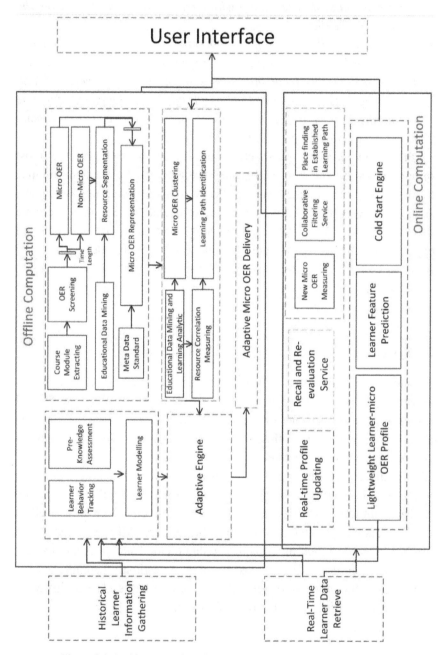

Figure 3.2 Architecture of Online and Offline Computation in MLaaS

3.5.1 *Offline Computation*

A. *Computational Services*

The Learner Modelling Service aims to build a specific model for each learner, on the basis of his/her historical information and ongoing learning behaviour. Learners' basic information about learning styles, preference and learning purposes is gathered from the Historical Learner Information Gathering Web service in the PLE. Based on these data collections, this service assesses the pre-knowledge level for each learner and marks up these features by a set of measurable variables. It is also provided with a function, which tracks learners' behaviours during micro learning process and ensures their models being kept up-to-date once new data are detected or generated.

The Learning Resource Representation Service stores all representations of the available micro learning resources. It extracts resource modules from well-developed OERs (e.g. MOOC courses). Based on their time lengths, they are categorized into micro learning resources (less than 15 minutes) and non-micro learning resources. Referring to the results of EDM and LA, these longer course modules are cut off programmatically and encapsulated into small units with reasonable time lengths. As this module holds a metadata repository, a metadata standard for describing micro course units is going to be established semantically (Veeramachaneni et al., 2013; Beydoun, 2009). According to this standard, all learning resources are represented in terms of discipline, key words, time length, language of instruction, popularity, difficulty and so on (Veeramachaneni et al., 2013). Data related to good-quality and mostly-followed/discussed learner-generated content, can be refilled into Learning Resource Repository in order to support peer-to-peer learning in MOOC (Beydoun, 2009).

For MLaaS, the Real-Time Learner Data Retrieve Service retrieves learners' real-time data, including their learning progress and current time availabilities (how many minutes they prefer to use in the moment).

Furthermore, in the Learning Resource Repository Service, selected course modules are clustered using text/data mining technologies. This service also measures correlations among chunks, or, if feasible, derives correlations from existing MOOC course modules. It helps to set learning start point and exit point and it also distinguishes the suggested sequences of learning resources and identifies a learning path among them.

Taking inputs from all the above services, the Adaptive Engine acts by providing learners with customized learning resources, which can match their current micro learning context, personal demands, learning styles and preferences. It is the core of the proposed system, which embeds machine learning technologies to realize the adaptive mechanism (Al-Hmouz et al., 2010; Bouyia & Demetriadis, 2012).

The MLaaS will also expose its functions over the mobile Web with a standard service-oriented architecture specification, and it is interoperable with other SaaS and Web services in the PLE.

B. Working Principle

Basically, the offline computation runs on a basis of compound transactions. When a learning activity launches, a compound transaction is generated associated with it, which can be therefore represented as:

{Learner Profile, Micro OER profile, Association},

where a learner profile and an OER profile are involved, linked by an association showing the learner's properties against the micro OER. Common OER delivery systems apply user ratings, preferences, click-through rates or popularities as explicit properties. Those systems usually adopt top-N recommendations so that a learner can have quite a few candidate learning resources. Unfortunately, according to a study in recommender system, very few learners cooperate in the rating process (Su et al., 2010). Thus, the offline computation is responsible to transform implicit user behaviours into explicit information (Sun et al., 2015).

A knowledge base acts as the think tank of the system and works behind the Adaptive Engine (Sun et al., 2017). Basically, the knowledge base is in charge of the semantic construction and storage of the learner profile and OER representation (Sun et al., 2017).

Adopting ontologies as the basis of the learner profile is crucial in addressing the cold start problem in micro OER delivery. It allows the initial learner behaviour to be matched with existing and pre-built knowledge in the ontologies and relationships among them. The semantic learner model will use a machine learning-based approach to acquire, represent, store, reason and update each learner's profile. It enables MLaaS to consider individual learning styles, learner's context, application capabilities, and teaching materials structure, leading to a customization of the type and delivery format of learning information in response to the user. Similarly, an augmented micro OER ontology will also be built, where every micro OER is measured in regards to its functional attributes and non-functional (QoS) attributes of the Web service it belongs to (Sun et al., 2015; Wang and Shen, 2016).

In the next Chapter 4, we will present a comprehensive learner model for micro open learning (Sun et al., 2015). This model involves features that can impact and constrain the micro learning experiences and outcomes, and is enclosed in an ontological representation (Sun et al., 2016; Sun et al., 2017). By taking advantage of the comprehensive learner model, the LearnerProfile can be broken down to:

{InternalFactors, ExternalFactors} = {IntellectualFactors & NonIntellectualFactors, ExternalFactors},

where the internal factors can be classified into personal intellectual and non-intellectual factors, differentiated by whether a factor is related to a learner's cognitive and intelligence level or not. External factors come from the environmental and social-economical contexts. Given the OER delivery has a 'big data' context, ideally there could be sufficient data sets to be used in data modelling and machine learning, and rule mining is compulsory to impute unknown values for online-prediction. Associate rule learning is adopted to realize the discovery process. In particular, multi-relation association rule discovery (Reza et al., 2014), context based association rule discovery (Shaheen et al., 2013), sequential pattern mining (Mabroukeh & Ezeife, 2010) and so on are employed. The detailed rule discovery strategy will be introduced in the Section 5.2. The rules can be represented as:

{LearnerProfile, MicroOERProfile}→{Association}

Technically rule mining and learner clustering operation runs throughout all the offline computation process. Therefore, the problem of missing values in collected data can be overcome without much difficulty.

As aforementioned, the core of MLaaS, namely the Adaptive Engine, processes the results from all other services and transmits its output to the user interfaces straightforward.

However, a big challenge appears in the real MLaaS applications. The initial MLaaS system has insufficient information about the learners, because both 'OER' and 'learner' are new to this emerging educational setting. This brings serious difficulties to launch the data processing work. The profile construction is not feasible without any information about the learner at the commencement of micro open learning.

C. Assembling Complete Micro Open Learning Experience

In a mobile service environment, it is feasible to utilize EDM and LA to identify micro learning resources which have similarities (Wang, 2008; Markellou et al., 2008). In addition, based on learners' historical learning records, the sequence by which learners go through resource chunks can be sorted out. In open learning, especially MOOC learning, various providers or universities may offer the same course with considerably different contents and section divisions. It is possible to learn cross several available course sections from different providers and synthesize such pieces to assemble a complete learning experience for a specific MOOC course.

There are strict sequences among some courses sections, which can be pre-defined by course providers (Tam et al., 2014). In other cases, sequences are just suggestive, and some learners can acquiesce in such sequences on the basis of others' recommendation and experiences if these are retrievable (Chen, 2008). EDM and LA can contribute to explore latent learning paths from historical cases and expose them to all MOOC learners.

There are many other ways that micro learning paths can be formalized via OER (Idris et al., 2009). The key considerations are that the learning activities should be short, available on-demand, or immediately relevant to a job task for employees.

Building and optimizing learning path are undertaken by the Learning Resource Repository Service, Concept title and description need to be extract from the concerned course materials manually. Thereafter, key words are worth to be extracted to deduce the importance of keywords through a document classification technique. The algorithms similar to the one proposed in the study (Matsuo & Ishizuka, 2004) could be utilized in our co-occurrence statistical information based keyword extraction. Assume that there are m keywords and key phrases in total being extracted from all n sets of course materials, an m-dimensional Euclidean space can be constructed accordingly. Each micro learning resource chunk can be parameterized as a keyword vector, which represents the corresponding concept in the m-dimensional Euclidean space, with each dimension representing the importance of a keyword in

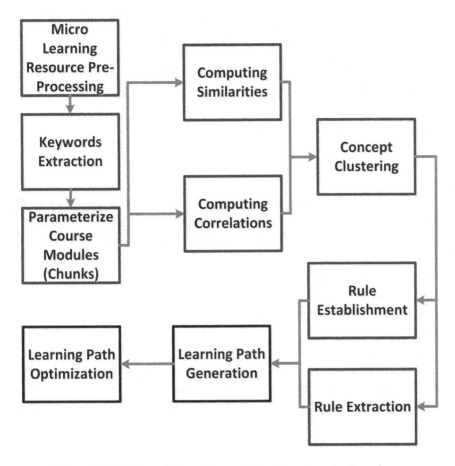

Figure 3.3 Workflow of Assembling an Entire Micro Learning Experience

the relevant course. Similarity calculation (e.g. Pearson correlation coefficient or the cosine similarity) will then be applied to measure the correlation coefficient between two resource chunks.

All course modules available in micro open learning can be clustered by using clustering algorithms, such as the widely used K-means and K-nearest neighbours, with their similarity metrics to categorize the course modules into different knowledge groups. Each cluster of course chunk is treated as an individual knowledge domain under the course. By leveraging EDM and LA, we can establish rules within each cluster or among various clusters to identify the sequence of two course modules.

Learning paths can be generated randomly as initial solutions, and then they are optimized by artificial intelligence techniques or heuristic algorithms (e.g. genetic algorithm) in terms of established rules and with respect to multiple purposes. The workflow of learning path optimization is shown as Figure 3.3.

3.5.2 *Online Computation*

The adaptation of online computation rises popularly in many industry-leading recommender systems, such as Netflix[b] and Amazon Online Store[c]. It is believed that online computation can respond better to recent events and user interaction, but has to respond to requests in real-time. This can limit the computational complexity of the algorithms employed as well as the amount of data that can be processed (Amatriain, 2013). It can effectively deal with data sets with comparatively smaller sizes. Inspired from the adoption of online computation in e-business and entertainment systems, we borrow the idea to facilitate the performance of MLaaS on the computation based on the 'recentness' of learning activities, namely learning behaviours and OER publishment.

The major contribution of the online computation domain we propose is that, it dedicates to handle the shortage of data (i.e. learning information) in building the initial learning model and path, due to the

---

[b] https://www.netflix.com/
[c] https://www.amazon.com/

both new system and new user conditions. It utilizes a lightweight version of learner-micro OER model to act on the pervasive cold start problem agilely. This lightweight model works in accordance with classification algorithms, similarity measures, and prediction techniques to figure out the problem of first delivery of micro OER without the requirement of any known priori probability.

Moreover, the online computation has expertise in promotion of new OERs by inserting latest published micro OERs into established learning paths. It also fuses the learners' nearest behaviours and most recent events into the recommendation results in order to meet the demand of high timeliness.

Summary

In this chapter we rolled out the 'big map' of our research and identified the research problems we will tackle in the upcoming chapters of this book. Firstly we reviewed the background of our research, where a PLE was proposed over a service-oriented architecture. Our pilot study motivated us to facilitate the current delivery shape of OER, and the research challenges were summarized in terms of adaptive micro learning, online computation and cold start problem, respectively. The research purpose was listed according to the sequence of upcoming chapters, and explained by scenario examples. In the Section 3.5 we described the system framework, where an online and an offline computation domain are involved to jointly make the decision of adaptive micro OER delivery.

Chapter 4

Comprehensive Learner Model for Micro Open Learning and Micro Open Learning Content

Following the system framework of MLaaS illustrated in the previous Chapter 3, in which the Adaptive Engines was introduced as acting as the core for the entire micro OER adaptation process, in this chapter we will concentrate on the theoretical design of a personalized learner model which underpins the operation of the Adaptive Engine. This model is oriented to the micro open learning and is based on a comprehensive review over literatures in computer science, information technology, pedagogy, psychology and social science areas. It aims to model the learner and learning context in an extensible manner with respect to the learning environment in space (i.e. mobile) and time (i.e. micro) manners.

This model contained features that affect the experience and outcomes of micro open learning. Its structure will be introduced in terms of the two domains of factors it consists of (i.e. internal and external): we will firstly investigate the personal factors come from the both internal sides which intellectually or non-intellectually reflect learning behaviours; and then, factors commonly found from the external circumstance will be identified.

The motivation to discuss the user (i.e. the micro open learning learner) and the item (i.e. micro open learning content) together is that, it allows consideration of individual learning styles and scenarios, device and application capabilities, and learning content structure, leading to customization of the type and delivery format of learning information in response to the user (Ahmed et al., 2010). Since the delivery options of learning resources in micro open learning is significantly increasing, there are quite a few factors functioning in the success of micro learning content delivery, in the Section 4.2 we will provide an overview of the learning content, namely micro OERs. Sequentially, the categorization and customization of OERs in the micro learning context will be described, along with the measurement of micro OERs.

4.1 Comprehensive Learner Model

Although it is not difficult to track, monitor and record the entire process of a learner who accesses OERs, reporting them visually and statistically in order to reveal each learner's learning story is more crucial. This plays a significant role in conducting study ratiocination, judging learners' study status, estimating learners' study progress and carrying out learning strategy decision making. Finally, a dynamic learner model for micro open learning can be established by using these screened and sorted data (Al-Hmouz et al., 2010), according to their historical and real-time data.

The data collection for building learner model can be realized in two ways: static data collection (e.g. from mandatory requests) and dynamic data tracking (e.g. from automatic extractions). The detailed learner features and learning context we intend to explore are listed in the following sections.

By investigating literature in the intersection of computer science and learning science, we have screened out features that play important role in the comfortability and success of micro open learning. As shown in Figure 4.1, the learner model consists of two domains of factors (i.e. internal and external), while the internal factors can be classified into personal intellectual and non-intellectual factors. Each domain is enclosed by a rectangle outline and is distinguished by a particular colour (i.e. external factors are in green rectangle, and internal factors are in black rectangle, where personal intellectual factors are in blue while Non-intellectual factors are in red). Some components can fall in the intersection of two domains which means these components are multi-correlated to two factors. Also, a component can be overlapped with others, which suggests that they are associated and mutually affected.

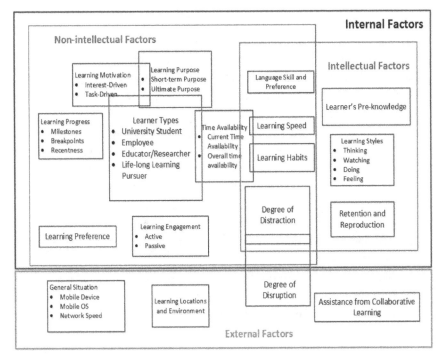

Figure 4.1 Comprehensive Learner Model for Micro Open Learning

4.1.1 *Personal Non-Intellectual Factors*

A. *Learner Types*

The types of open learning learners vary evidently in accordance with their particular learning purposes and work, and life patterns. Their background information, though not always, can be searched from their registration and logon data (DeBoer et al., 2013; Kay et al., 2013). Some common types are:

- Full time students in universities who prefer to learn distantly and electronically rather than attend lectures in person. They are willing to enjoy the convenience brought by the smart and portal devices.
- Full time university students in developing countries where education is lower-developed. Because of scarce learning resources from their own universities, open learning gives them greater opportunities to remotely participate in classes provided by leading universities so that

they can make step forward their daily learning and appreciate the advanced knowledge management and teaching approach.

- Educators who work in universities in developing countries. They take OERs to obtain experiences from leading universities as well as learn how to teach in an efficient way to improve their own teaching approaches and flows.

- Researchers who are following up the flow of OER delivery (e.g. MOOC courses) to explore potential defects in them, which result in barriers for learners to get knowledge passed on. Their goals are to refine the current OER teaching flows and to look for enhancing teaching approaches in a virtual manner. During the progresses when they are engaged in open learning, pauses are frequently made, and several specific sections of courses are retrieved repeatedly in terms of research demands.

- Employees who are required by their corporations or organizations to take OERs for training purposes. Commonly they have a concentrate timeframe to complete OER learning. Their overall learning schedule is driven by their trainers and they have freedom to complete their allocated tasks continuously and arrange their time for each specific course units in place.

- Employees who wish to enrich their knowledge or improve their skills by taking OERs in their off-work hours. Their final target is to become more competitive in workplace and they are generally self-motivated. Hence, they set targets and milestones for each learning period by themselves with relatively more freedom and autonomy.

- Life-long learning pursuers. They can be employees whose open learning contents (e.g. MOOC courses) may not be closely related to their daily work, or they may be non-working persons such as housewives, elders or retired people (Blaschke, 2012). Generally these kind of open learning learners are interest-driven (Cochrane et al., 2012).

B. Time Availability

Learners' disposable time varies to a great extent, which is highly indicative for whether and how often these learners would adopt micro learning modes. Thus, their current time availability is better to be set as a mandatory request for them to input before they start each micro learning activity.

C. Learning Engagement

Anderson et al. argues that the more engaged learners got higher marks in their MOOC courses. Most of their findings depend on analyses of students' participations and publications in the education forums provided with MOOC platforms (Anderson et al., 2014). They state that more engaged learners show more frequently in forums and are very positive to raise questions and attract other learners' interests to join their discussion regarding the learning contents. It does not mean they are lower-performing learners and contribute less in forums to seek useful advices and experiences, while the lowest-engaged learners even do not appear in the forums.

Past studies (e.g. (Milligan et al., 2013; Alario-Hoyos et al., 2014)) used quantitative methodologies to identify individual learner's engagement in open learning and categorize them into cohorts in different ways. However, there lacks a unique definition for the extent of engagement of a learner. It is mainly measured in terms of a learner's total online time length, frequency of login, submission of required assignments, participation in forums, completion of courses or course chunks, etc.

Learners' engagement can also be categorized into active or passive learning. The former refers to that learners are self-motivated to attend virtual classes in MOOC platform so that they look for and initiatively access open learning resources, which they need when they want; while the latter refers to that learners act as recipients of knowledge through information pushed by MOOC platforms or MOOC affiliated social medias, for example, they might have subscribed electronic reading materials.

D. Progress Identification

This is basically identified by breakpoints and milestones made by learners. In micro open learning, learning activities become disperse, and the contents in two continuous learning phases can be not rigidly restricted in accordance with the sequences in the course curriculum. Learners' learning progress is not only confined into particular time points, but also categorized by taking their learning recentness into account. (Bruck et al., 2012)

E. Learning Motivation and Purpose

Basically in open learning learners are either interest-driven or task-driven. There learning purposes are identified by mandatory request data which means learner are suggested to input their learning purpose prior to the commencement of their open learning.

F. Learning Preference

Learning preference refers to learners' subjective and affective opinion about learning contents. It can be sorted out through learners' comments and tags made on resources they have accessed.

4.1.2 Personal Intellectual Factors

A. Learner Pre-knowledge Assessment

To build a profile for each learner and customize micro learning strategy for learners with different backgrounds and basis, a measure that is necessary to take in prior is to assess each learner's background knowledge in terms of several standards. In micro open learning, it is suggested to investigate and identify their pre-knowledge level in terms of the extent of their education, their historical courses grades in MOOC, and results of pre-course quizzes which are easy to be quantized.

A typical measure adopted by many e-learning systems is the pre-knowledge assessment (Xu et al., 2014) which refers to taking exams before learners commencing their courses. Although this is common to organize in on-campus courses, it is not feasible to directly migrant this into micro open learning as learners are more distributed and on-the-go.

The outcomes of the pre-knowledge assessment are easy to be quantized. Hence, in micro open learning, it is suggested to investigate and identify their pre-knowledge level in terms of:

- The extent of their education. This can give a general image of a learner's academic background and capabilities of acquiring new knowledge.
- Their historical courses grades in MOOC. This is to find learner's performance in related courses in order to build a reference to predict at what level s/he can commence a new course.
- Results of pre-course quizzes which are often in the form of multiple choices. It does not increase the difficulty of operation on mobile devices.

B. Learning Styles

Individuals differ in how they learn. Learning styles refer to the systematic differences in individuals' natural or habitual pattern of acquiring and processing information in learning situations.

According to the study conducted by Kolb and Kolb (Kolb & Kolb, 2005), learning styles can be represented as concrete experience (feeling), reflective observation (watching), abstract conceptualization (thinking) and active experimentation (doing). However, because operations on mobile devices are relatively simple, which are limited in input and output methods, these four learning styles are difficult to be reflected straightway through monitoring learners' operation. Thus, identifying learners learning style requires extra efforts. For example, some external approaches are feasible to employ, such as self-evaluation. In addition, if learning activities in other open learning activities are specified in terms of relevant learning styles, learners' performance in an exact learning activity can indicate their values on the corresponding learning styles.

C. Memory Ability

Memory ability can impact learning outcomes after the retention and reproduction stages of learning (Bui & Myerson, 2014). For OERs in the disciplines of culture, literature, arts, language and history, etc., memory ability is one of the key measures that can help learners transfer the contents of online OERs into their own knowledge. It is particularly important when learning these disciplines using fragmented time pieces (Xiong, 2015).

4.1.3 *Intersection of Non-Intellectual and Intellectual Factors*

A. Learning Habits

Each individual learner has a completely isolated structure of available time and learning time. Learning times for on-campus instructor-led learning mostly falls in day time. Unlike that, the mobile/micro open learning time spread over all 24 hours of the day. Their personal situations affect their learning habits, which refer to, in this research, how learners utilize their time on open learning, in what way they get learning resources passed on, how often they make pause and repetition, after how long they take a review, whether they learn OERs offered from several providers in parallel, during what time stages in a day they are more often to make open learning happen, and among those time stages, when they are more often intending to adopt micro learning means.

B. Learning Speed

This feature refers to the extent that learners spend in going through a course chunk and finishing related tasks on average. It can be estimated from their historical learning records.

C. Language Skill and Preference

Learners' language skills and preference should be taken into consideration to opt in/out their learning resources. Because most OERs are in English so that identification for learners' level of English skills is essential. Alternatively, this service investigates whether they are preferred to learn in their native languages or another second languages other than English.

D. Degree of Distraction

Internally it concerns a learner's mood and emotion, and it is highly correlated to the degree of disruption, which is a component of the external factors (Dennen & Hao, 2014; Khaddage et al., 2015).

4.1.4 *External Factors*

A. *Learning Locations and Environments*

The ways how learners get connected to Internet apparently reveal their learning locations and surrounding environments. Generally in micro learning scenarios, they are brought to Internet through wireless networks by two means, namely Wi-Fi or mobile cellular network (e.g. 4G, 3G, and GPRS). Simply, connecting to internet through mobile network means learners are taking on learning activities ad hoc, the strength changes of the mobile signals can reflect their statuses of being on-the-go. The logon data of Wi-Fi portal may also determine learners' exact indoor learning places. Normally connecting Internet via Wi-Fi provided in public places rather than homes indicates learners are possible to experience higher frequency of interruptions as their surrounding environments can be more noisy and complicated.

B. *General Situation*

General situation regarding learning context partially affects their learning experiences and achievements. Information regarding the mobile devices and mobile OSs the learners utilized to carry out micro open learning must be specified in order to determine devices capabilities, features and limitations (Tortorella & Graf, 2012).

C. *Assistance from Collaborative Learning*

Encouraged by the nature of how open learning is structured and OERs' pedagogical concept, learners can get helpful information from P2P learning which can be collaborative learning, virtual social activities over social network and assimilating knowledge from content generated by other learners (Ji et al., 2016).

D. *Degree of Disruption*

The degree of disruption depends on the noise and interference factors from their surroundings, conflicts with their daily works, comfortableness with the setting and layout of the OER delivery platforms, course design and so on (Christensen, 2003).

4.2 Micro Open Learning Content

4.2.1 *Micro OER Categorization and Customization*

A. *Ready-made Micro OERs*

Open learning has changed the expectation of learners and the technologies that support open learning can also support micro learning. Now that open learning has expanded, in both size and format (i.e., OERs have evolved and now the acronym encompasses many different types of courses), OER providers offer several options for training departments or education providers and agencies to implement micro learning paths within an organization, and for learners to build up their own learning schedule with full of varieties and joys (Lourdes & Albert, 2013). Some typical learning resources involve short videos and other visual learning resources, spaced repetition and practice activities, communication and collaboration environments, and credentials and gamification. Therefore, if micro learning resources are well-defined within short time length (i.e. 15 minutes), they are normally delivered right away.

For these well-designed resources, specific EDM schemes can be developed to establish a recommendation model for students in similar situations in the future, for grouping web documents using clustering methods in order to personalize e-learning based on maximal frequent item sets; for providing personalized course material recommendations based on learner ability and to recommend to students those resources they have not yet visited but would find most helpful (Romero & Ventura, 2010).

B. *Non Micro OERsz*

However, most achievable MOOC contents are non-micro learning resources, which need to be refined properly. These contents need further processing and revision to fulfil micro learning demands, which can be instructor-led or computer-based.

The ultimate shapes of resources after processing are summarized as follows:

- Visual encyclopedia: Learning key points are listed out in terms of the knowledge structure of the entire course. For each key point, a video or textual material is set up without time limit to clearly illustrate the self-contained content. Because the content contained solely cover a particular scale, accordingly the required learning time is short.

- Logical segmentation of courseware and course videos: Herein each unit covers the complete in-formation of a learning section, which includes the conditions of beginning and end, carries coherent contents, and can be studied individually.

- Extraction of sections from a complete course material: In this case the specific knowledge parts are selected and extracted in the first place while the redundant contents of the course are eliminated. Given many OERs with the same contents or knowledge scopes are offered from different OER providers, (e.g. a MOOC course 'machine learning' offered from Stanford University and Carnegie Mellon University) the section extraction enables learners to learn in parallel, precisely locate the particular chapters, with no need to go through the whole course.

- Course-related and educational information in affiliated social media: This is a ramification of learning resources and also has rich educational values. This resource can be found not only in forums or blogs embedded in MOOC platforms, but also in other popular social media (e.g., Face-book, WeChat, Twitter, Tumblr, etc.), where learners, educators or external experts publish course-related materials (Mark et al., 2010). A noticeable feature of this kind of resources is that its amount increases from time to time while some of the contents may contain pseudoscience or incorrect information (Dowling, 2013; Henry, 2014).

- Subscription learning: from pedagogical view it is also been deemed as passive learning. As its name implies, it provides an intermittent stream of learning-related interactions to those who are subscribed. These learning-related interactions can involve a great variety of learning-related events, including content presentation, diagnostics, scenario-based questions, job aids, reflection questions, assignments, discussions, etc. Such interactions are short, intentionally scheduled over-time to support learning, often utilizing research-based findings related to the spacing effect. Learners subscribe one or more series of learning interactions can form as multiple learning threads (Waard et al., 2012).

- Two-way interactive contents or activity settings, ranging from feedback, assessment, review for contents generated by other learners, peer-to-peer learning, cooperative writing, collaborative work, and flipped classroom.
- Learner-generated contents: highly promoted by open learning practitioners and educators, P2P learning, digital flip classroom, mutual supervisions are more and more of attached educational values in open learning (Lee & McLoughlin, 2007). The new shape of MOOC which emphasis connectivist brings the acquisition and sharing of learner-generated contents into regular learning means (Cochrane et al., 2013; Narayan, 2011).

4.2.3 *Micro OER Measurement*

A. *Functional Attributes*

For modelling purpose, a learning resource chunk is considered to be measured with regards to the following features (Al-Hmouz et al., 2010; Miranda & Albano, 2015; Bouarab-Dahmani et al., 2015):

- Time length
- Suitability for mobile learning
- Didactic model (inductive, deductive, learning by practice, etc.)
- Mediality (e.g. print media, electronic media, mono-media vs. multi-media, (inter-)mediated forms, etc.)
- Difficulty (level of knowledge)
- Completeness
- Requirement of attention
- Preferred learning styles
- Type of interaction (expositive, active, one-way imparted or two-way interactive)
- Requirement of input or hands-on practice
- Learning type: repetitive, activist, reflective, pragmatist, conceptionalist, constructivist, connectivist, and behaviourist; also: action learning, classroom learning, corporate learning, etc.

Also, a micro OER has its basic information such as topic, discipline, serial number, language it is taught, etc., which will be treated as the input of adaptation algorithm as well.

B. Non-functional Attributes (QoS)

These attributes describe the quality of services enclosed in the OERs system. We carry on the typical standards used in service-oriented architecture, and listed some typical attributes that have more important influence on the delivery and user experience of micro OER (Alama & Ahmad, 2016). These attributes involve:

- Performance (response time, latency, downtime, throughput)
- Reliability (availability, fault tolerance, recoverability)
- Robustness and stability
- Scalability and sustainability
- Compatibility, interoperability and adaptability
- Security

This part of responsibility is jointly taken over by an external service from main provider. MLaaS invokes its output and makes decision in conjunction with the adaptive results.

Summary

In this chapter we have presented the structure of a comprehensive learner model which focuses on the most significant inputs that impact upon and constrain the micro-learning experiences. The learner model consists of two domains of factors (i.e., internal and external), while the internal factors can be classified into personal intellectual and non-intellectual factors, differentiated by whether a factor is related to a learner's cognitive and intellectual levels. Some components fall in the intersection of two domains, which means these components are correlated to both factors. Also, associated components are overlap with others. Learners' data will be gathered to construct the learners' profile.

The semantic construction of the learner model will use a machine learning-based approach to acquire, represent, store, update and infer (with the Adaptive Engine) each learner's profile. It allows the system to consider individual learning styles, learner's contexts, application capabilities, and teaching materials structure, leading to a customization of the type and delivery format of learning information in response to the user. The detailed approach will be introduced in the next Chapter 5.

Chapter 5

Semantic Knowledge Base Construction: Education Data Mining and Learning Analytics Strategy

Since all decisions of micro OER adaptation are made by the Adaptive Engine, it acts as the core of the offline computation system. It consumes the results from all other services and transmits its output straight to the user interfaces. For this reason, the MLaaS is conceived to meet the standard of a data-rich system, and a knowledge base serves as its think tank. Basically, the knowledge base is constructed using a top-down approach, by making use of semantics means, from the pattern level to data level. In other words, several ontologies are drawn at first, followed by 'data processing' work. We attempt to combine the pattern and rule discovery processes of micro learning with a survey of the education literature to produce features that could affect the learning experience and outcomes in a mobile environment (Sun et al. 2015). In detail, 'data processing' work involves all operations on data, from the very beginning to the end, such as entity extractions, relationship extractions, resolution disambiguation and so on.

Given that we have the overall system framework in place (refer to the Chapter 3), we consequently adopt a conceptual graph-based approach for dealing with the ontology construction (Starr & de Oliveira, 2013; Xu et al., 2011). These graphs profile the features that play a significant role in an ongoing micro learning process, and also depict how features were mutually affected by and interrelated with each other. According to our design, the profiling procedure is carried out from two sides, the learner side and the OER side.

While the profiling proceeds forward, some new problems appear which contradict our original design intentions. One of the most important problems is that the system, MLaaS, knows little about the learners, because either 'OER' or 'learner' is new to this emerging educational setting. This creates serious difficulties for commencing the 'data processing' process. Profile construction is impossible with insufficient information about the learner at the commencement of open learning. Therefore, the learner profile cannot be fully filled in with valid data.

The research focuses on the knowledge base for micro OER recommendation and delivery. Naturally, based on the volume of retrievable data, this problem can be approached from two sides.

- If a learner is well-known by the MLaaS, an educational data mining and learning analytics (EDM and LA) approach will be applied to his or her historical data to understand his or her learning patterns and preferences. Thereby, a well-grounded recommendation can be made based on his or her personalized settings and particular surroundings. This will be in charge of the offline computation domain of MLaaS, and this will be presented in this chapter.

- If a learner is relatively poorly known by the MLaaS, (i.e., this is a new learner to the open learning environment), this will be treated as a cold-start problem and tackled by filling in the gaps with predicted data, so that a recommendation will be made based on demographic information. The cold start problem will be addressed in the next Chapter 6.

- Freshly generated information, along with the cold-start recommendation, will populate the first version of a learner's profile.

5.1 Conceptual Graph-Based Ontology Construction for Micro Open Learning and Proposed Data Processing Strategy

Generally, a workable knowledge base has a two-tier structure: a pattern level at the top and a data level at the bottom (Cambria et al., 2014). For the pattern level, the ontologies are constructed based on conceptual graphs. By this means, the ontologies represent the formal dimensions of the data processing workflow, and can drive data processing with a priori knowledge, thereby reducing the search space (Xu et al., 2011; Dou et al., 2015).

By accomplishing a comprehensive survey of literature in the fields of pedagogy, psychology, e-learning and mobile learning, we sorted out features that might play key roles in the micro open learning experience and achievement. These conceptual graphs also represent how features were affected by and interrelated with each other in the ongoing micro open learning process. This will be introduced in the subsequent sections, from the OER (item) side and learner (user) side, respectively.

5.1.1 *Augmented Micro OER Ontology*

From the item-based perspective, we deepen the sights from normal e/m-learning into the micro learning environment. For this reason, the general ontology of OER is augmented to adapt the needs of micro learning.

In an augmented micro OER ontology, an annotation of a micro OER is self-describing; with metadata exploring its educational parameters, such as typology (video, audio, text, etc.), type of interaction (expositive, active, mixed, two-way), didactic model (e.g., inductive, deductive, learning by doing, etc.), and non-functional attributes, such as QoS, semantic density and so on (Miranda & Albano, 2015). Each node in an augmented OER ontology indicates a micro OER chunk. A chunk is the smallest unit in the micro learning settings—normally a finely-cut piece of an OER from its provider—with an apparently shorter time length (preferably less than 15 min) than its original shape. It can be a mini concept or knowledge point, tinier than what teachers used to deliver; or it can be a cut of course video or lecture notes; or course settings delivered along with a concept, such as assessment, task, reading material and so on (Sun et al., 2015).

No chunk is totally independent, and each of them is part of a relational web rather than merely a conceptual object (Moreno et al. 2013). This ontology is used to explicitly classify the OERs for recommendation among a pedagogically defined set of distinctive main concepts, fed as the raw material into the reasoning process of MLaaS (Sun et al., 2016; Moreno et al., 2013).

A conceptual graph of the augmented OER ontology is shown as Figure 5.1.

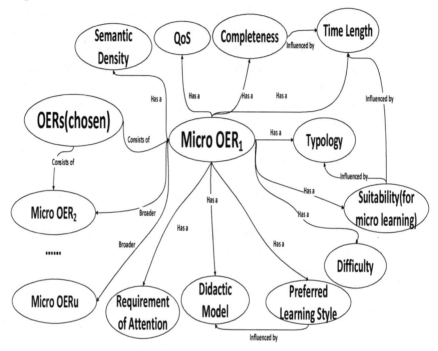

Figure 5.1. Conceptual Graph of Micro OER Ontology

5.1.2 *Augmented Micro Learning Learner Profile Taxonomy*

From a user-based perspective, the main ontology, on which all learner profiles are based, is named the Benchmark ontology, where the element Learner is put at the centre of the graph (Sun et al., 2016). Acting as an instance of a pre-set domain ontology, a specific learner profile oriented to micro learning is a set of nodes from the Benchmark ontology matched with a node in the augmented micro OER ontology. It contains plenty of annotations in terms of their learning behaviours and context. A conceptual graph of the benchmark ontology is shown as Figure 5.2.

Figure 5.2. Concept Graph of Benchmark Ontology for a Learner Profile in Micro Open Learning

5.2 EDM and LA Strategy

5.2.1 *Methodology*

Student learning data collected by open learning systems are being explored to develop predictive models by applying educational data mining methods that classify data or find relationships. These models play a key role in building adaptive learning systems, in which adaptations or interventions based on the model's predictions can be used to change what students experience next or even to recommend outside academic services to support their learning.

Analysing these new logged events requires new techniques to work with unstructured text and image data, data from multiple sources, and vast amounts of data ("big data"). Big data does not have a fixed size; any number assigned to define it would change as computing technology advances to handle more data. So "big data" is defined relative to current or "typical" capabilities. For example, Manyika et al. (2011) defines big data as "Datasets whose size is beyond the ability of typical database software tools to capture, store, manage, and analyse." (Manyika et al., 2011)

At this cutting edge, educational data mining and learning analytics are widely used to research and build models in several areas that can influence online learning systems. As its name implies, EDM is 'a state-of-art that applies the data mining techniques to educational data' (Romero & Ventrura, 2010). It is concerned with many developing methods, and acts on exploring the unique types of data in educational settings. Using these methods, students and the settings in which they learn can be better understood (Romero & Ventrura, 2010). To enable smart and adaptive micro learning for MOOC, EDM and LA are key concepts that we employ to build the basis of the dynamic learner model construction.

5.2.2 EDM and LA Stakeholders

EDM and LA not only can help learners personalize their micro open learning and recommend them activities, resources and even people they may have similar interests and targets to join as cohorts, but also can be of great significance for open learning instructors and OER providers.

For open learning instructors, EDM can help to get objective feedback about instruction; to analyse students' learning and behaviour; to detect which students require support; to predict student performance; to classify learners into communities or groups; to find a learner's regular as well as irregular patterns; to find the most frequently made mistakes; to determine more effective activities; to improve the adaptation and customization of courses, etc.

For OER providers and open learning participant universities, EDM can help to enhance the decision processes; to streamline efficiency in the decision making process; to achieve specific objectives and enhance competitiveness among all OER providers; to suggest certain courses that might be significant for particular groups of learners; to find the most cost-effective way of improving retention and grades; to admit learners who will do well in open learning and attract more learners to engage in, etc.

5.2.3 EDM and LA Strategy

Reporting learners' data visually and statistically to demonstrate their unique learning story, and also their learning constraints (such as time availability), is crucial. This plays a significant role in assessing learners' study status, estimating learners' study progress, and carrying out strategic decision-making. This process is responsible for the benchmark setting for routine data extraction from the open learning platform.

For the bottom level (i.e., the data level) of the knowledge base, the technical operation of semantic learner profiles and knowledge base construction for micro open learning is based on data that populates the graphs from two sources: explicit data collection (e.g., through mandatory requests); and implicit data tracking (e.g., automatic extraction) (Moreno, 2013).

In addition, rather than developing the domain ontology for OERs by ourselves, a general structure of courseware ontology is built jointly by making use of existing ontologies, which were extracted from major OER providers, such as universities involved in major open courseware alliances (e.g., participating institutions in edX[a], or from the Linked Open Data Cloud community[b]) (Capuano et al., 2009).

The investigation of 'big' open learning data is related to OER. Among the massive OERs, three main types of relations are foreseen:

- ConsistsOf is an inclusion relation. This relation can be generally found between two OERs or one OER and one micro OER. Two items with this relation are located in different hierarchies of the augmented micro OER ontology.

- RequiredSequence is a strong order between two items (OER or micro OER), where the former micro OER must necessarily be learnt before

---

[a] https://www.edx.org/schools-partners

[b] http://lod-cloud.net

the latter one, due to course settings and educational consideration.

- RecommendedSequence is a weak order between two items (OER or micro OER), where the former micro OER is suggested to be learnt before the latter one, according to the instructor's guidance, but is not mandatory.
- It is certainly possible for two items (OER or micro OER) to have no relation at all.
- Both relations regarding sequence can be inherited by entities' descendants, for example, if there is a RecommendedSequence (R_1, R_2) indicating an OER R_1 is preferably learnt prior to R_2, then, for $MR_1 \in R_1$ and $MR_2 \in R_2$, there is a RecommendedSequence (MR_1, MR_2).

The purpose of the EDM/LA is to amend, enrich and validate the aforementioned ontologies built manually and extracted semi-automatically, and verify and weigh the importance of discovered relations. Our combination of EDM and LA is realized on the basis of two components (Markellou et al., 2005); on-campus mobile learning data (i.e., structured data), and 'big' open learning data (i.e., unstructured data). In particular, we are carrying out the experimental EDM and LA by conducting a substantial analysis of the real data of learning behaviours of students from a public university in Australia. The data are collected from the main learning management system (LMS) and data warehouse of the university. This analysis aims to identify the regular patterns of students getting involved in blended learning (i.e., on-campus learning and e/m learning); for example, whether and how often they adopt micro learning modes to accomplish learning tasks, to explore the major factors that affect their learning habits, and most importantly, to understand the rules for the ways in which features listed in the personalized learner model are mutually affected by, interrelate with, and act upon their learning outcomes. At this stage, we are discovering potential trends, which cannot be directly shown from the data we have gathered. We can then apply such findings to open learning scenes and infer what is behind the scene. The detailed data sets are illustrated in Table 5.1:

Table 5.1. EDM and LA Data Sources from University Warehouse.

Data Type	Purpose
Learners' exact time of logon/out for each time	To know how long they stay online each time
The IP address or gateway information of their internet connection	To know their exact learning location and surroundings
Mobile device information, mobile operator information and mobile OSs	To know their general situation
Their personal enrollment information (full time or part time, nationality)	To know their learning time availability, organization and language skills
Their residential information (session address and permanent address)	To understand their distance to campus and the potential modes of transportation they adopt)
Subjects they have chosen (current)	To know their academic background and field
Subjects they have chosen (historical)	To know their academic background and field
Historical grades	To know their academic background and infer level of pre-knowledge
Course materials they have accessed (material type, topic, length, requirement associated with them)	To know their learning habits (how they prefer learning resources to be passed on)
Course requirement/milestones set in LMS (by instructor)	To know the suggested learning schedule
Their detailed learning activities (What they do when staying online and how long they spend on each specific learning activity, type of resource they access for each specific time)	To know their learning habits, learning engagements, learning speed and so on.

Their interactions with LMS and learner-generated content (from forum and thread, etc.)	To know their preferences, interests and to measure their engagement.
Frequencies of their participation in interactive learning activities (e.g., forum, thread)	To know their engagement
Extent of completeness for each learning activity	To know whether they finished an entire step of learning or drop off halfway
The learning paths they have gone through (the sequence of their access of learning resources over LMS)	To further establish optimal learning paths
Their learning achievement (grades and final marks if possible)	To know how their learning behaviors, affect their learning outcomes
Groups or teams they have participated in	To know their collaborative learning performance and similarities/changes of learning time frame among learners

Based on the prospective EDM and LA result, a meta-data standard is built which functions in digitalizing and formalizing the description of learner behaviours and external factors. It is responsible for the benchmark setting for the routine data extraction from open learning platform. The study is subsequently extended and applied to a larger scale, by analysing 'big' data from real open learning activities. Data mining means with different aims are shown in the first column of Table 5.2.

Table 5.2. EDM and LA Scheme for Open Learning Data.

Technique	Object	Purpose
Prediction	well-defined micro OERs	to establish a recommendation model for students in similar situations in the future

Structure Discovery	well-defined micro OERs	for web documents using clustering methods in order to personalize e-learning based on maximal frequent item sets
Latent Knowledge Estimation	Non-micro OERs	to discover which stages of them are generally finished within relatively larger time length
Structure Discovery	Non-micro OERs	to determine time spans where the pauses made by learners usually fall in
Factor Analysis	Non-micro OERs	to find out the actual reasons why learners spent more time on these stages and made such pauses
Latent Knowledge Estimation	Non-micro OERs	to measure potential suitability of micro learning (from learners' frequencies of using fragmented time pieces)
Factor Analysis	Non-micro OERs	to identify resources' suitability for micro learning, for example, whether hands-on practice is needed, or whether the OER delivery is necessarily associated with lots of writing or computation work which is inconvenient to complete on mobile devices
Prediction	Subscription OERs	to determine when to push information to learners in the best timing and remind them
Clustering	All micro OERs	to determine their correlations for better repository purpose
Relationship Mining	Time Availability	to discover the correlation between their overall time availability and learners' types

Clustering/Prediction	Time Availability	to involve similar learners into cohorts and build a potential time frame for their overall learning schedule
Latent Knowledge Estimation	Learning habit (learning time distribution)	to discover whether there are regular patterns of time organization within time frame among learners in or across cohorts
Latent Knowledge Estimation	Learners' latest learning contents and activities	to retrieve and profile learners' learning recentness
Categorization	Learning habits	to set up a unique learning habit summary for each learner
Relationship Mining	Learners' learning location data	to know the degree of distraction and how it interrelates to disruption from external environment
Relationship Mining	Learners' mobile app usage	to know the degree of distraction and how it interrelates to disruption from the content on mobile internet
Social Network Analysis	OERs in affiliated social networks	to distinguish information that can be useless, harmful and may cause time wasted for learners.
Social Network Analysis	Other content in affiliated social networks	to screen well-recognized information in order to recommend to learners as their learning augmentation besides the OERs (text mining technique employed)

To a considerable extent, the establishment of the data level can involve integrating heterogeneous OCW repositories, refining and blending available OERs into the micro learning context and publishing their metadata as linked data. Because in recent years some educators and researchers have made great efforts to publish and popularize the OER in terms of the linked data concept, a workflow developed with this extended aim is generally divided into six phases:

1. Identify and select heterogeneous data sources to determine the scope of the content.
2. Model vocabularies for OER domains.
3. Data extraction.
4. Generate standardized data descriptions (e.g., RDF data).
5. Publish linked data.
6. Consume and display linked data.

Summary

In this chapter we have presented the construction of a semantic knowledge base that underpins the decision-making process of the micro OER recommendation system which is realized by the Adaptive Engine. The knowledge base was built using a top-down approach based on conceptual graphs, by having two augmented ontologies at the pattern level first. Using this, a strategy on processing data was then developed at the lower level. This EDM and LA strategy is to understand micro learning patterns and rules, from the both on-campus data and open learning data perspective, and to support the decision-making process of the micro OER recommendation system.

Chapter 6

Online Computation for MLaaS

In this chapter the operation procedure of the online computation domain of MLaaS will be introduced. As the benefit stated in the Section 3.3.3, The adoption of online computation aims to tackle the nearline activities the can reflect the 'recentness' of the learning behaviours and act on the fast response of micro OER recommendation.

Furthermore, the adoption of online computation is expected to improve the performance of MLaaS in the following aspects:

1. Given the complete newness of the MLaaS as well as the new coming users who have no record on the micro open learning, the focus of this chapter is to make the first delivery to learners in their fresh micro open learning journal. This is realized by the functionality of addressing cold start problem in the online computation.
2. For newly published micro OERs, it is central to their acceptance and popularity that it can be discovered and collected in recommendation list as soon as being released. This requirement will be fulfilled by a heuristic mechanism that inserts the newly published micro OERs into established learning paths.
3. The online computation is also in charge of making up limitation in timeliness and renewal of the offline computation by keeping the comprehensive learner model and learner-micro OER profiles up-to-date.

The above three aspects will be introduced in the upcoming Section 6.2, 6.3, and 6.4 in sequence.

6.1 Lightweight Learner-Micro OER Profile for Cold Start Recommendation

6.1.1. *Augmented Micro Learning Learner Profile Taxonomy*

As discussed in the Section 4, based on a comprehensive survey in the literature of pedagogy, psychology, e-learning and mobile learning, we have classified out features that might play key roles in the micro open learning experience and outcomes. From the user-based view, such a comprehensive learner model is annotated by semantic approach. These ontologies also represent how features affected and interrelated with each other in the ongoing micro open learning process. As the instances of the pre-setting domain ontologies, a specific learner profile oriented to micro learning is a set of nodes root from the main 'comprehensive learner model' ontology versus a node in the augmented micro OER ontology. It contains plenty of annotations in terms of their learning behaviours and context.

To technically operate the semantic learner profile for micro open learning, data collection comes from two sides, the explicit data collection (e.g. through mandatory requests) and implicit data tracking (e.g. automatic extraction) (Moreno et al., 2013).

6.1.2. *Representation of Lightweight Learner Profile*

Although from the item view, it is feasible to get micro OERs measured in terms of the standard defined in the micro OER profile; from the user view, it is unlikely to have such sophisticated information in hand with a null history of a fresh learner, so that, in many cases, the learner model oriented to offline computation lacks sources to activate.

Despite low adoption in education area, the lightweight model based recommendation, for example rating based recommendation, is a good alternative for intensive data maintenance approaches needed by ontology-based recommendations in offline computation (Nadolski et al., 2009).

Hence, this cold start condition motivated us to simplify this comprehensive learner profile described in the Section 4 to a lightweight version. It merely deals with necessary information for decision making in order to act on the initialization agilely (Luz et al., 2013).

The lightweight learner profile is managed by MLaaS with two parts: the static part and the dynamic part. The static part can be represented by a vector, which contains the demographic and educational information. By matching these two augmented ontologies, for item and user respectively, the dynamic part of a learner node is denoted as a pair, $L_j=$ $\{MR_u, ML_j\}$, $L_j \in L$. Herein, the element MR_u denotes the uth micro OER, which is a particular version of the micro OER ontology, as introduced in the Section 4, and a three dimensional element ML_j $\{P_{u,j}, TA_j, D_j\}$ is exclusive to j^{th} learner during the micro learning process. Herein, the element $P_{u,j}$ indicates the learner's preference, TA_j indicates the jth learner's instant time availability, and D_j denotes the level of distraction in terms of the given learning environment and surroundings.

Each of these three features proposed in the lightweight profile is associated with a confidence degree to reflect its subjective relevance. For example, if an explicit information is provided by the learner directly and appear as a number rather than a range, its associated confidence degree is set to full.

Whenever MLaaS gathers any information from the learner's learning process over OER, the learner profile will be updated in regard to ML_j.

6.1.3. *Instant Time Availability*

The system is able to obtain explicit information on how long the learner can (or would like to) spend on a micro OER through mobile devices in the real time. As a mandatory request, a learner is required to input his or her instant time availability at the beginning of every micro learning activity.

According to the system setting, suggestively the instant time availability, TA_j, is represented by an integer from 1 to 15. However, if the learner is not sure how long s/he is able to spend on the micro OER at once, s/he is free to leave a time span, which can be continuous integers in the same range.

6.1.4. *Preference Propagation*

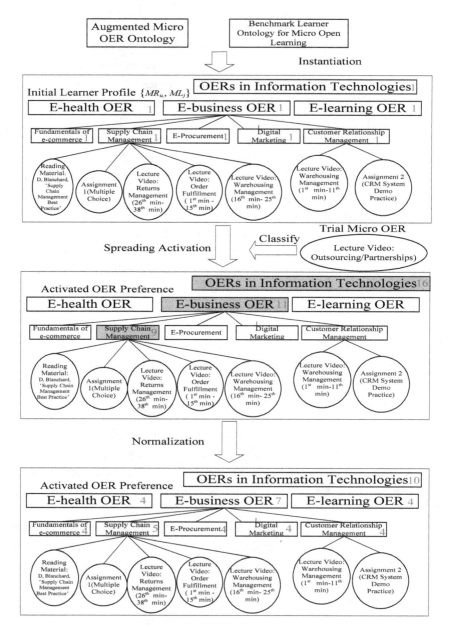

Figure 6.1 Partial View of the Augmented Micro OER Ontology and Spreading Activation for a Learner's Preference on OER

Given the cold start condition for the first micro OER delivery, a learner is required to quickly mark down a preference on a specific micro OER. Consequently, a spreading activation approach is applied to maintain the preference against its parent node (i.e., the R_v is the vth OER where the MR_u derived from) as well as updating learner profile. It propagates the learners' preference upwards the hierarchy of micro OER ontology based on activation values. In other words, the preference has been obtained from a micro OER to its ancestor and spread in its superclass (i.e., OER) level. An example of the spreading activation is shown in Figure. 6.1.

A partial view of augmented micro OER ontology in 'information technologies' area is shown in Fig. 2. Particularly, it describes an 'e-business' OER from an Australian provider, OpenLearning (www.openlearning.com). At the bottom level of the ontology, the nodes depicted with oval shape typically conform to the standard of micro OER. The red integers shown in nodes with rectangle shape are preference values from a learner versus target OERs. The Algorithm 6.1 is proposed to execute the process of preference propagation.

Algorithm 6.1: Preference Propagation

Input: *Dynamic part of learner profile L_j ={MR_u, ML_j }, a trial micro OER MR_u, $L_j \in L$*

Output: *Updated dynamic part of learner profile with updated $P_{u,j}$ value in the triple dimensional set ML,*

   $P(R_v)$ and Activation(R_v), preference value and activation value for the OER R_v

---

//Step 1: Spreading Activation
begin: *Initialize PriorityQueue;//PriorityQueue is the set of OERs within the same discipline where R_v belongs to*
   Set Activation of all micro OER to 0
   for each *$L_j \in L$* **do**
         if *($MR_u \in R_v$)* **then**
            Activation(R_v)= $P(R_v)$
            PriorityQueue.Add(R_v)
         end if
   end for
   while *PriorityQueue.Count >0* **do**

Sort PriorityQueue; //activation values in descending order
Select the first item MR_u in PriorityQueue // R_v with highest P value
Remove R_v in PriorityQueue
    for each R_v do
    LinkedOERs=GetLinkedOERs(R_v)//get linked nodes of R_v
        for each R_w in LinkedOERs do *//propagate activation to its*
        neighbors
        Activation(R_w)+=Activation(R_v)*Weight(R_v, R_w)
        PriorityQueue.Add(R_v)
        Sort PriorityQueue
    end for
    end for
end while
    //Step2: Learner Profile Normalization
for each $L_j \in L$ **do**
P(R_v)= P(R_v)+ Activation(R_v)

$$k =1/ \sqrt{\sum_{t=1}^{v}(R_v)^2}$$ *//normalization factor*

P(R_v)= P(R_v)*k //normalization
$P_{v,j}=P(R_v)$
    end for
end

The normalization factor acts on preventing the propagated preferences from escalating continuously to such an extent that exceeds a reasonable range, which could result in difficulty of data processing in the forthcoming process. The confidence degree for the propagated preference of OER is recorded as *CD ($P_{v,j}$)*.

6.1.5. Distraction Prediction

A. Demographic Classification

In the Chapter 4 (Sun et al., 2015), we discussed the key issues that might cause distraction in micro open learning, which generally came from two sides, the social side and environmental side.

In addition, MLaaS investigates existing learners' degree of distraction as reference, and senses every learner's location information through built-in functions in mobile devices. Based on the given taxonomy and augmented ontology, we carry out a demographic classification that aims to cluster learners into cohorts, in order to match them with micro-pieces of OERs (Sorour et al., 2016).

The mechanism of classification is designed as, learners who have similar static information, involving employment and/or education background, occupation, and similar learning environment/location, are more likely to experience a similar level of distraction. For the same reason, their overall time availabilities would more likely fall in the same range. Herein MLaaS tries to associate a learner into a pre-clustered learner group, by applying the stereotyping technique to fulfil the requirement of demographic classification.

For a newly joined learner, L_j, an ensemble method of a binary classifier and a one-against-all model is utilized to obtain multi-class classification (Milgram et al., 2006; Galar et al., 2011), in order to predict its category, C_j. The system is trained with existing set of learners, L. Typical binary classification techniques, i.e., C4.5 decision tree (Kotsiantis, 2007; Polat & Gunes, 2009) or Naive Bayes classifier (Dalton & Dougherty, 2013) can be employed to serve as the base algorithm (i.e. training algorithm F in Algorithm 2 described below) in order to produce a suitable classifier, CF_k. A new learner L_j is classified with the label k, whose CF_k produces the highest value of $\hat{y}$. Please note the $\hat{y}$ refers to the value of the objective function of the one-against-all classification.

Provided that the L_j is categorized into its corresponding category C_k, the L_j's neighbourhood, NB_j, is then calculated by the Algorithm 2. This aims to match a new learner's category with an existing learner's category.

The Algorithm 6.2 shows the process of demographic classification.

Algorithm 6.2: New Learner Classification and Neighbourhood Calculation

---

Input: Sample (the current learner set L), Labels y (where y_i is the label for a sample learner L_i and $y_i \in \{1,2,...K\}$), Training Algorithm F, the new learner set N

Output: Set of neighbors, NB_j, of a new learner L_j

---

begin:

    // *Build an ensemble method of a binary classifier and a one-against-all model*

    for each k in {1,2,...K }**do**

        set a new label vector z_i for y_i,

        if *(y_i=k)* **then**

            $z_i=1$

        else

            $z_i=0$

        end if

        $CF_k=F(L,z)$ //*use binary classification technique to produce classifiers*

    end for

    //*Use multiclass classifiers to categorize new learners*

    for each $L_j \in N$ **do** // *L_j is a new learner*

    $\hat{y} = \arg\max_{k \in \{1,2...k\}} CF_k(L_j)$

    end for

    output C_j =k // C_j is the category of the new learner L_j

    for each $L_j \in N$ **do**

        set NB_j=null

        Predict C_j // L_j's category

        for each L_i in L **do**

        Retrieve C_i

        if $C_j == C_i$ **then**

        Add L_i to NB_j

        end if

        end for

    end for

end

Hence, the demographic classification is realized according to learners' static and location information. Once new learners join into the open learning scenario, MLaaS responds immediately to classify them into clusters.

B. Similarity Measure between Two Learners

MLaaS is responsible to find the similar existing learners in the discovered demographic categories, so as to recommend them micro OERs that were recognized as suitable to learn in a given time span, situation and environment.

Learners' learning location information is sensed from the location service embedded in the mobile devices. Thus, the similarity between two learners, L_i and L_j, is evaluated using the equation (1). Please note the L_j is a new learner and L_i is one of his/her neighbour.

$$sim^L(i, j) = [(\sum_{l=1}^{m} S_l W_l)^2 + (SLo_{i,j} W_{i,j})^2]^{1/2} \qquad (6.1)$$

where S_l is the similarity value of the lth attribute in the static part of learner profile and the W_l is its corresponding weight. $SLo_{i,j}$ denotes their similarity on location and $W_{i,j}$ denotes the weight for location factor.

C. Distraction Prediction

The prediction of distraction starts at once a new learner accesses MLaaS. The approach introduced in Section 5.5.1 applies firstly in the new learner clustering.

Then, in terms of the equation (2), the distraction value can be estimated in accordance with the action that any member, L_i, in the same cluster with L_j, indicates the predicted distraction level.

$$D_{j,Lo_a} = \frac{1}{2} * (\frac{\sum sim^L(i.j) \bullet d_{i,Lo_a}}{\sum sim^L(i,j)} + d_{j,Lo_a}) \qquad (6.2)$$

where $d_{j,Loa}$ is the self-identified degree of distraction the learner L_j felt in the location Lo_a, acquired by mandatory request. This follows the expectation that the learners who have a similar general situation (i.e.

social factors) and surroundings (i.e. environmental factors) are in high probability to have a similar degree of distraction, and the disruption levels come from the same location are not do not vary considerably.

The confidence degree for the predicted distraction is depicted as $CD(D_{i,Loa})$.

6.2 Online Computation Process for Cold Start Problem

6.2.1. *Integration of Recommendation Results-Cold Start Problem*

A. Downwards Propagation

In Section 5.4 we have obtained the preference of a learner on an 'entire' OER rather than on a micro OER, now the preference values are again propagated downwards the ontology hierarchy. Consequently, each micro OER node receives an estimated preference value from its ancestor. This propagation process is executed with a decay factor. For each micro OER the final preference value, $P_{u,j}$, can be calculated using the following equation (3).

$$P_{u,j} = \frac{\sum P_{R,j}CD\ (P_{R,j}) + \sum P_{v,j}CD(P_{v,j})Q(u,v)}{\sum CD(P_{R,j}) + \sum CD(P_{v,j})Q(u,v)} \quad (6.3)$$

where R is the set of all the nodes in the higher hierarchy than MR_u, R_v is a direct ancestor of node MR_u and $Q(u,v)$ depends on the count of level between MR_u and R_v.

$$Q(u,v) = L(|\,uv\,|) = \begin{cases} L(0) = 1 \\ L(l) = (1-\lambda)L(l-1) \end{cases} \quad (6.4)$$

and the confidence degree for the descendant node, in regards to the $P_{u,j}$, is calculated as the average of the confidence values in its ancestors, decreased by a decay factor, μ.

$$CD\ (P_{u,j}) = \frac{\sum CD\ (R)}{|R|} - \mu \qquad (6.5)$$

As far as all values of the three attributes, namely denoting preferences, instant time availability and degree of distraction, in the set *ML* are settled, a lightweight learner profile is completely constructed from the initially scarce information by the MLaaS.

A. Micro OER Screening and Rules

For each micro OER, once MLaaS has acquired its final preference value and confidence degree, those nodes, which do not meet the minimum requirement of confidence degree, is rejected by the system.

When generating a list of recommended micro OERs, the ones with higher learners' interests are placed at the top. For two micro OERs MR_u and MR_w, their sequence is determined according to some heuristic rules which are defined in accordance with the extraction of three types of relations discussed in the Section 4. These rules are executed sequentially with priority.

1. If there is a RequiredSequence relation between these two micro OERs, the prerequisite one is placed above (refer to the Section 4).
2. If the preference regarding these two OERs, $P_{u,j}$, $P_{w,j}$, the former one is higher than the latter one, then the MR_u is above MR_w
3. If, in the absolute terms, the confidence degree $CD(P_{u,\,j})$ is high and the $CD(P_{w,j})$ is low, then the MR_u is above MR_w.
4. If there is a RecommendedSequence relation between these two micro OERs, the one which is suggested to be accessed first is placed above (refer to the Section 4).
5. The micro OER, which is more related to the learners' education background, or falls in the relevant disciplines or inter-disciplines is placed with priority if the disciplinary difference between this two candidate micro OERs is obvious.
6. Otherwise the recommended micro OER list is randomly ordered if none of the above rules applies.

Herein, the first rule is deemed as a hard rule which should be strictly obeyed, and the rest rules are soft rules which can be violated with educational consideration, from case to case.

C. Optimization of Recommendation Results

MLaaS consumes the value P and D in conjunction with their TA to compare with the attributes and requirements annotated in the metadata of the augmented OER ontology.

The next step is to integrate the outcomes from the previous algorithms described in above Sections; a fitness function will convert these selected multidimensional arrays, (i.e., numerical values of features proposed in the lightweight profile) into one variable. Hence, this problem is hereby properly transformed to a multi-objective optimization problem.

The basic idea of the ultimate micro OER recommendation is that, given each recommended micro OER serving as the commencement of micro open learning is supposed to be followed by a series of micro OERs to form a complete learning path, we name it as the first object in a learning path. For this reason, to initiate the constrained multi-objective optimization, candidate learning path solutions (chromosomes) are randomly generated where each of them is a learning path with a series of micro OERs, rather than an individual micro OER. For a chromosome, its violation degree is investigated by examining the relations between each contiguously prior/posterior micro OER pair against the first 5 rules listed in the previous Section 6.1.2, and then summing up. For such pair in a chromosome, its violation degree, $VD(MR^t, MR^{t+1})$, is calculated by the weighted sum of its violations against rule 2 to rule 5, respectively, where MR^t is the tth micro OER in k and MR^{t+1} is the $t+1^{th}$. The higher the violation degree is, the more serious the candidate's learning path violates the rules. The violation degree of a candidate learning path, k, is calculated using the following equation (6):

$$VD_k = \sum VD(MR^t, MR^{t+1}) \qquad (6.6)$$

Thereafter, let the variable RA_u denote the degree of required attention of a given micro learning resource, MR_u, whose real-time suitability for micro learning, $RT_{u,j}$, is calculated by comparing with the learner, L_j's predicted distraction, using the following equation (6.7):

$$RT_{u,j} = \{(RA_u)^2 + [CD(D_{j,Lo_a}) * D_{j,Lo_a}]^2\}^{1/2} \qquad (6.7)$$

Hence, for the candidate learning path, k, RT_{kj} denotes the sum of the real-time suitability of micro OERs it contains. Similarly, P_{kj} sums up all the predicted preferences from the learner L_j versus micro OERs that k contains.

$$\eta = \min(\alpha VD_k + \beta RT_{k,j} + \gamma / P_{k,j}^1 + \delta / P_{k,j}) \qquad (6.8)$$

where α, β, γ and δ serve as weight for each variable and suggestively $\alpha > \beta > \gamma > \delta$, P_{kj}^1 denotes the L_k's preference value of the first micro OER in the candidate learning path k.

The algorithm 6.3 illustrates typical steps in making the first recommendation.

Algorithm 6.3: Micro OER Recommendation in a Cold Start Condition

Input: $P_{u,j}$ (the Learner L_j's predicted reference to the micro OER MR_u), $D_{j,Loa}$ (predicted distraction level), $CD(P_{u,j})$ and $CD(D_{i,Loa})$ (their confidence degree), RA_u (the degree of required attention of MR_u), TA_j (the instant time availability), rules (1st-6th)

Output: the tag of a micro OER which acts as the first delivery

begin: Randomly generate candidate learning paths as chromosomes
    for each chromosome k **do**
        Select all micro OERs it contains
    for each MR_u in a chromosome k,
        Calculate its $P_{u,j}$ and $CD(P_{u,j})$.
        Import $D_{j,Loa}$, $CD(D_{i,Loa})$ and RA_u
        Calculate its $RT_{u,j}$
    end for
    Calculate k's VD_k
    Use equation (8) to evaluate its fitness η

---

end for
while *iteration times < max iteration time* **do**
    apply heuristic approach to generate new candidate solutions
    for each *new chromosome k' **do***
    check time length of the first micro OER in k', $TL_{k'}^l$
        if *$TL_{k'}^l$ is in the range of TA_j*
            keep k'
        otherwise
        reject k'
        end if
    evaluate the fitness of k', η, using equation (8)
    end for
    replace chromosomes with higher η
end while
    output the selected N chromosome k'' with minimum η and
    satisfied $TL_{k''}^l$
    select the first micro OER in each k'' as the first delivery
end

The heuristic Algorithm 6.3 infers a list of suitable micro OERs as the first attempt of learning resource recommendation for a learner at the commencement of the novel micro open learning experience via MLaaS.

Along with the successful launch of a solution to the well-known cold start problem in micro learning, learners' upcoming behaviours will be continuously gathered by MLaaS to feed the Adaptive Engine in the offline computation.

6.2.2 Insertion of New Micro OERs into Established Learning Path

A. Optimization of Micro OER Similarity Calculation

To some extent, the insertion of new micro OERs into well-established learning path can be seen as a new item cold start problem. Hereby, the similarity calculation among micro OERs is crucial to the quality of item-based collaborative filtering approach (Airoldi et al., 2012). Using the equation (9), this calculation is not only based on their Euclidean distance on educational settings, but also added a time decay factor, which considers accumulation and attenuation of interest, and a penalty term, which tackles the filter bubbles. These two operators are shown as the latter multipliers in equation (6.9).

$$sim^M(n, g) = \sum (\mid n, g \mid) * N_0 e^{-\lambda(t_1 - t_2)} * \frac{1}{\log_a(O_j + c)} \qquad (6.9)$$

where the t_1 is the current time and t_2 is the time when the existing micro OER, MR_g, was released. O_j refers to the times of L_j's operation, retrieved from the real-time MLaaS usage (as stated in Section 4). The constant c keeps the denominator unequal to zero.

As introduced in Section 6.1, an established learning path is exclusive to a specific learner, e.g. L_j, whose preference values in the matrix are selected. A K nearest neighbour (KNN) algorithm is able to cluster items with higher similarities with the new micro OER, MR_n. Its neighbors form as a set, G (Airoldi et al. 2012). Consequently, the new micro OER preference prediction is calculated by the following equation (6.10):

$$P_{n,j} = \overline{P_j} + \frac{\sum\limits_{g \in G} sim^M(MR_n, MR_g) * (P_{g,j} - \overline{P_j})}{\sum\limits_{g \in G} sim^M(MR_n, MR_g)} \qquad (6.10)$$

B. Inserting New Micro OERs into Established Learning Path

After identifying the neighbors of MR_n and predicting L_j's preference onto it, a hill-climbing algorithm is employed in the approach to locate the appropriate place for the MR_n. The new items will be inserted into established learning paths according to the Algorithm 6.4:

Algorithm 6.4: Insert New OER into Established Learning Path (New Item Cold Start Problem)

Input: MR_n (a newly published micro OER), G (the existing micro OER set, and $MR_g \in G$, Established learning paths, Semantic Relationships of OERs (as defined in the Section 5)

Output*: Optimized learning paths which contain the MR_n inserted at the suitable position*

begin*: Investigate the MR_n in terms of measurements as described in the Section 4.*

Measure its similarities with existing micro OERs using equation (6.9)

Use KNN algorithm to cluster MR_n's neighbors

//Let G denote the set of neighbors of MR_n

MRn's semantic relationships among neighbors in G are firstly examined according to the standard provided in Section 5.

Invoke established learning paths or use the Algorithm 6.3 to produce candidate learning paths

for each** MR_g ∈G **do

select learning paths that contain MR_g

cut a segment that contain MR_g and few micro OERs prior/ posterior to it in each learning path

//find the rough positions where the MR_n might be located at

for each** segment **do

MR_n's semantic relations among micro OERs in the few places are examined again

***if** there is a 'RequiredSequence'*

locate the place for MR_n

interposition it between the micro OERs according to this strong order (as introduced in the Section 5)

end if

***if** there is a 'RecommendedSequence'*

put MR_n among the micro OERs according to this weak order

or

put MR_n in parallel with one of existing micro OERs alternatively

compare the predicted preference values of MRn and all existing micro OERs' in this segment

apply the rule 2 in the subsection B of the Section 6.3.1

measure the fitness of new learning paths using equation (8)

> *use Hill Climbing algorithm to compare fitness*
> > *replace an existing OER in established learning path with worse fitness*
>
> **or**
>
> > *insert MR_n between two existing micro OERs, keep MR_n added on as extra if the fitness is satisfactory*
> > *//in this case the overall quantity of items in the new learning path is increased*
> > > **end if**
> > **end for**
> **end for**
> > *generate new learning paths containing MR_n*
> **end**

It is notable that the Hill Climbing algorithm performs on the comparison of fitness can effectively abandon the learning paths with poor fitness by searching locally and reduces the times of iterations. This accelerates the overall speed of generation of learning paths with new micro OERs inserted.

This approach does not examine throughout all elements in all matrices, hence its computing complexities and running time are acceptable for online computation which is in demand of fast response.

6.3 Real-Time Complementary Mechanisms

The online computation copes with users' near-term and real-time activities which have not been sorted in historical data repository. In addition to the 'new user' cold start problem solving, it also holds a real-time algorithm in a 'second' granularity, from the item view. This comes with two considerations. The first is to improve the recommendation performance over the micro OERs newly published, especially on the same day of that the learner access the MLaaS. Further to the approach introduced in the Section 6.2.2, it can increase the discoverability of new micro OERs even though they do not have any popularity or rating data recorded in the system. In addition, the most recent operations on a micro

OER can reveals its recommendation value more correctly. As the online computation should respond in seconds, redundant offline algorithms need to be simplified considerably as the time is absolutely not allowed to examine through all learner-micro OER interactions.

The algorithm simplification can be carried out by either row extension or column extension, or both, to the learner-micro OER matrix. Its major outcome is to update the profiles and the comprehensive learner model. The updating is not supposed to be executed at full-scale at the online computation side, while it is with clear purpose and highlight the 'recentness' of operations.

For the column extension, the online computation domain inquires and retrieves a specific learner's recent micro open learning behaviours, which is the list of the micro OER the learner has accessed in a very recent period. The corresponding names of the micro OERs in those usages are then filled into the 'item' columns to complement the gap in the learner-micro OER matrix which has been horizontally expanded beforehand. This can eliminate the gap between new and old micro OERs, and solve the problem that the breadth of correlations among micro OERs cannot be split. It also acts on eliminating effects to the offline computational results caused by the correlations among old micro OERs which haven't been accessed by the specific learner in the near- or real-time.

For the row extension, the online computation domain targets on a specific micro OER and invoke the list of users who are accessing it in the real time. The corresponding names of the users in those access logs are then filled into the 'user' rows to complement the gap in the learner-micro OER matrix which has been vertically expanded beforehand. However, the correlations in depth and breadth varying associated with the row extension is able to be split. In other words, the online computation and offline computation can be conducted separately, and there is not any data gap. Hence, technically it makes less sense than column extension.

Summary

When both the system and users are new, the lack of initial learner information in MLaaS brings difficulties to the commencement of adaptive micro open learning as well as MLaaS operation.

In this chapter we introduced a novel approach to deal with the cold start problem in the recommendation of micro OERs. We primarily focused on the online computation construction against the sparsity of data.

Our main contributions can be summarized as: we identified the cold start problem and innovatively adopted the degree of distraction as a reference index to make recommendation, associated with learner preferences. Sequentially, a detailed approach was provided to tackle the cold start problem by predicting these selected features in a mobile environment with fragmented time frames from the initial little-known information. Augmented semantic profiles of OERs and lightweight models of learner-micro OER were built accordingly to model the structure and features of learners' and micro OERs' information. Based on the above works introduced in the Section 6.2, a workable heuristic algorithm based approach was also presented in the Section 6.3.1.

Moreover, we also addressed the 'new item' cold start problem by coming up with a solution to insert newly published micro OERs into established learning paths, which was solved by the Algorithm 6.4. This algorithm was enhanced by a Hill Climbing approach to reduce the search scale.

Lastly, the approach illustrated in the Section 6.3 aimed to keep the comprehensive learner model up-to-date and enable the responses to learners being in second granularities.

Implementation and Empirical Evaluation

Since the design and computation process of MLaaS have been detailed in previous chapters, in this Chapter 7 we will present the implementation and empirical evaluation for this research. At the beginning, we will roll out the topology and working principle of the MLaaS in the Section 7.1. Following that we will evaluate the performance of the computation process in the Section 7.2. Algorithms for cold start will be executed first to identify the ideal size of top N recommendation, and pick up the optimized heuristic to serve as the core algorithm. The chosen algorithms will be consequently compared with established recommenders presented in literatures.

7.1 System Implementation

7.1.1. *System Topology*

The topology of MLaaS is shown in Figure 7.1. As a data-rich system, MLaaS will be able to exploit detailed learner activity data not only for recommending what the next micro learning activity for a particular student should be, but also for predicting how that student will perform on that future learning content.

In a pilot work of our team (Sun & Shen, 2013), we proposed peer-to-cloud and peer-to-peer models for resource sharing and storage in service-oriented contexts. Such models can have higher upload and download speeds than a traditional cloud model, user model or peer-to-server-peer model, and can be more robust to the failures of peers or servers in the cloud environment (Sun & Shen, 2013; Shen et al., 2011). Hence, we adopt this design and apply its concept as the topology of the new system for micro open learning.

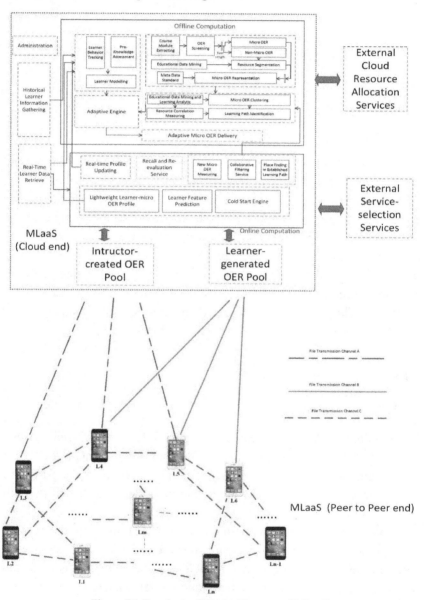

Figure 7.1 Topology of the Architecture of MLaaS

The P2P sub-network of the proposed system is to conform with the nature of open learning, where varieties of P2P learning occur frequently and randomly. This P2P tier guarantees that P2P learning can be organized instantly, and the first-hand resources can be shared and exchanged straight away, regardless of access to the cloud.

From the top-down view, MLaaS borrows the cloud service to maximize the capability of hosting. The cloud part of the system consists of four domains: data tracking, data collection, data processing and data storage.

The functions of modules in MLaaS's cloud-end were outlined in the Chapter 3 (Sun et al., 2015; Sun et al., 2015). An Administration Service is added to oversee the daily regular operations over MLaaS, from both learner and provider sides. A noticeable feature of the system is that there are three file transmission channels:

- A channel between learners and an instructor-created OER pool in the cloud storage part (i.e., the Channel A in the Figure 7.1).
- A channel between learners and a learner-generated OER pool in the cloud storage part (i.e., the Channel B in the Figure 7.1).
- A channel among all learners engaged in open learning (i.e., the Channel C in the Figure 7.1).

Once a learner indicates his or her desire to carry out micro learning and sends such a request from a mobile device, OERs will be transmitted through one of the three channels.

Where the OERs actually come from the cloud resources pools (i.e., from which exact cloud nodes the OERs are retrieved and invoked) will be defined and externally supported by third-party service-selection and resource-allocation services from mainstream service providers. This problem has been well studied; typical solutions can be found in the work reported in the work presented by Wang and Shen (2016).

Architecture and technical details of MLaaS can be referred to the Chapter 3 and Chapter 6. It is worth noting that MLaaS only produces micro OERs, rather than OERs. That is to say, normal OERs available online are collected by MLaaS and clustered in the OER pools, as shown in Figure 7.1. For this reason, despite MLaaS owning its data collection mechanism, it shares some demographic and educational data with the platforms or providers from which the OERs originate. This helps in learner profiling, which was introduced in the Chapter 5, even if a new learner registration in MLaaS is informal, and without sufficient demographic and educational data provided, as introduced in the Chapter 6.

7.1.2. *Working Principle of Adaptive Engine and Operation Environment of MLaaS*

The working principle of the Adaptive Engine which is located in the offline computing domain is shown as a sequence diagram, i.e., the Figure 7.2.

It is worth noting that there could be a need to merge the recommendation results obtained from both the online and offline computation. Since we adopt the Top-N recommendation, hence the recommendations provided from both side will appear in the recommendation list in a pro rata way.

To cope with the thoughts raised in the Section 3.1.3, ideally a cloud environment is configured for the operation of the PLE, namely the combination of TaaS and MLaaS. TaaS has been programmatically developed and deployed over the famous Amazon Web Service (AWS) cloud infrastructure. As aforementioned in the Section 3.5, MLaaS is naturally service-oriented and performing in company with the previously-developed TaaS (Sun & Shen, 2014). MLaaS emphasis interactions with OER providers' platforms and educational institutions' learning management systems, and it exposes its functions for those systems as well as external services (e.g. service-selection and resource-allocation services) to call and then invoke.

Consequently, to implement the service-oriented framework in a mobile cloud environment, and to minimize the cost and time of development, it is worthwhile to employ the AWS again to fulfil the requirement of hosting, storing, computing and mobile-enabling. In this case, series of cloud services provided by AWS work in conjunction to

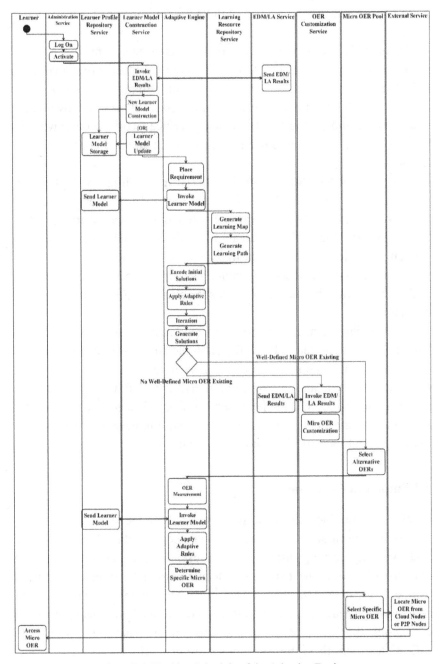

Figure 7.2 Working Principle of the Adaptive Engine

build the comprehensive peer-to-cloud/peer environment for micro open learning.

Technically, the cloud hosting part is taken charge by the Amazon elastic cloud computing (EC2), in which the EC2 block storage volumes (EBS) hold an instance for the entire system, comprising the extensible demand of CPU, memory, storage and network affiliated. Meanwhile the Auto Scaling and Elastic Load Balancing services work together with the EC2 Container service in order to adjust its volume and control internet traffic.

The information MLaaS deal with is snowballing with the fast-generated data (i.e. from both historical and real-time sides) regarding OER production and learners learning behaviours in open learning. AWS Import/export Snowball is ideal to utilize to addresses common challenges with large-scale data transfers including high network costs, long transfer times, and security concerns. Amazon S3 will be employed as the data storage because of its robustness and mature disaster recovery mechanisms.

Considering the interior of personalized learner model for micro open learning, it is suggested to be deployed in the Amazon Rational Database service profiting from its resizable capacity in terms of real-time demand of data extraction and inference. Finally, the P2P tier of MLaaS is mapped out using Mobile Hub service from Amazon, which allows learners to create a personalized link and send it to peers for fast resource exchanges and transmissions through Channel C.

7.2 Empirical Evaluation

Firstly we introduce the data sets we used in the evaluation of our approaches discussed in this paper. Note there is almost no e-learning system using learning distraction as a user rating, and because of the domain difference, the experimental data cannot be directly borrowed from existing data sets, such as the famous MovieLens. As a result, 3055 course samples are crawled from three main MOOC providers. Given we are among the first practitioners to apply micro learning concept into MOOC learning, these course samples are generally not in micro mode.

We did not technically segment every course sample longer than 15 minutes into smaller pieces, while tagging each piece of it with starting time and end time. For example, the 'Supply Chain Management' course video in an 'e-business' OER from an Australian provider, OpenLearning, has an original length of 38 minutes. Instead of technically clipping it into three chunks, the three virtual micro OERs derived from it are attached three sequential tags in their corresponding MicroOERProfile sets and come with time tags '1-15 min','16-25 min' and '26-38 min', respectively. After logical segmentation, the final size of the trail micro OER sets is 11407. The RA value of each micro OERs is derived from the course level settings identified by its provider, basically a course is in any of the five Grade Levels: Primary, Secondary, Further Education (diploma, college and technical schools), Higher Education (undergraduate) and Postgraduate. Moreover, each OER can have a Level of Study, which can be an Introductory Unit, an Intermediate Unit or Principal Area of Study, an Advanced Unit or a Specialized Advanced Unit, with the order of increasing difficulty. By jointly considering both types of levels, and applying a normalization calculation, The RA values are manually set for all micro OERs, ranging from 1-10.

1400 user profiles are randomly generated conforming to the law of normal distribution. Their demographic data component is fully filled. Most users' data regarding behaviours over micro OERs are left as blank, while very few users are set up with initiate values in their dynamic parts of lightweight profile, serving as seed data.

Next, for weights in the Subsection B of Section 6.1.5, W_l is set as 0.8 and $W_{i,j}$ is set as 0.2; for weights in the Subsection C of Section 6.2.1, α, β, γ and δ are set as 0.4, 0.3, 0.15 and 0.15, respectively.

Researchers investigated the performance of the binary classifier C4.5 decision tree and Naïve Bayes classifier, using MovieLens data sets, while C4.5 produced results with better Mean Absolute Error (MAE) or Root Mean Square Error (RMSE) (Lika et al., 2014; Sieg et al., 2010). Therefore, we adopt the C4.5 in Algorithm 2. The evaluation of the demographic classification illustrated in Chapter 6 is carried out on the basis of a classic k-fold cross-validation approach.

7.2.1. Empirical Study 1 - Evaluation of Heuristic Recommendation for Cold Start

In e/m-learning area, high MAE and RMSE values do not equal to high user satisfaction. In Top-N recommendation the Precision and Recall are suggested to be utilized as evaluation indices because they are more user-centric.

To obtain the scale of relevant micro OERs in the simulated data set, the heuristic algorithm is executed four times.

1. For the first time, the exact Algorithm 6.3 is executed; a Top N recommendation list is generated.
2. For the second time, the exact Algorithm 6.3 is executed, a Top N+2 recommendation list is generated.
3. For the third time, the preference feature is removed from the fitness function in Algorithm 6.3, a Top N+2 recommendation list is generated.
4. For the fourth time, the distraction feature is not considered in algorithm operation, a Top N+2 recommendation list is generated.

We take the results obtained from the first time of algorithm operation as the exact recommended items. As the rest algorithm operations return larger solution sets than the first time, the union set of the latter three Top N+2 lists is treated as the relevant micro OER set.

Table 7.1 Recall and Precision Definition

	Relevant	Irrelevant
Recommended	True Positives (TP)	False Positives (FP)
Non-recommended	False Negatives (FN)	True Negatives (TN)

Recall. The Recall value is defined as the relevant micro OERs recommended by MLaaS versus all relevant micro OERs, where:

$$R = \frac{TP}{TP + FN} \tag{7.1}$$

Precision. The Precision is the proportion of recommended items that are relevant to the given context, where:

$$P = \frac{TP}{TP + FP} \tag{7.2}$$

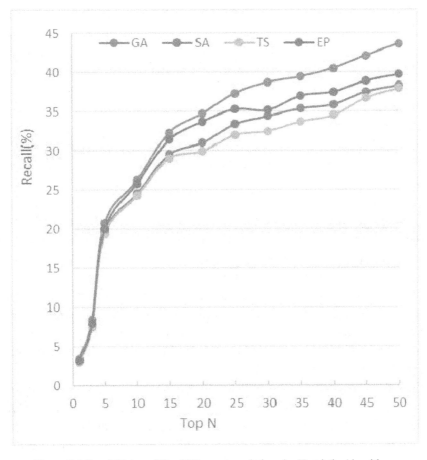

Figure 7.3 Recall Value of Top N Recommendations by Heuristic Algorithms

For the heuristic algorithms proposed in the Algorithm 6.3, four heuristic algorithms, namely Genetic Algorithm (GA), Simulated Annealing (SA), Tabu Search (TS) and Evolutionary Programming (EP) are selected to conduct the computation. In Top-N recommendation, different numbers of recommendations shown in the list might lead diverse performance. We also investigate the impact of the value of N on the performance of recommendation. We set N as 1, 3, 5 and thereafter every multiple of 5 till 50. The experiment results are shown in the Figure 7.3 and Figure 7.4.

As shown in Figure 7.3 and 7.4, each heuristic algorithm provides acceptable Recall and Precision results initiated from a cold start condition. Almost all of them reach the convergence after 250 iterations, which is in a reasonable scale. It is notable that when N is set larger than 15 the Recall values do not increase sharply. GA gains the highest Recall value while the rest are all between 35% and 45%, which does not incur a major difference.

As shown in Figure 7.4, although EP performs best at the beginning of comparison, its performance drops dramatically when N is set larger than 15.

GA could be an alternative as it shows more stable performance. Combining both indices together, GA holds a better Recall-Precision values overall. However, it can be argued that if the learner prefers a concise list of recommendation, EP is worth to be considered as the core algorithm. Turning back to the micro open learning scenario, it is ideal to have the higher Recall and Precision values the better. Briefly, the higher Recall values give the learners opportunities to go through wider range of micro OERs in terms of the given context (Lu et al., 2015). However, in micro OER recommendation, poor precision can lower the user satisfaction as if learners fail to get their wanted resources at the first time they may choose to switch off. Hence, when these two indices cannot be fulfilled at the same time, it is suggested the Precision value has higher priority (Sikka et al., 2012). Also, this conforms with the feature of mobile devices, as a screen smaller than 5.7 inches is generally not capable to provide dozens of candidates for use at a glance. If a learner is required to turn to the next page many times at the first time of MLaaS access, the user satisfaction can be negatively impacted as well

(Son, 2016). Therefore, an insight can be derived that when setting up the recommendation list, the number of candidates is not suggested to be exceeding 15. Please note in the Figure 7.3 and 7.4, GA, SA, TS, and EP are the abbreviation of genetic algorithm, simulated annealing, Tabu search and evolutionary programming, respectively.

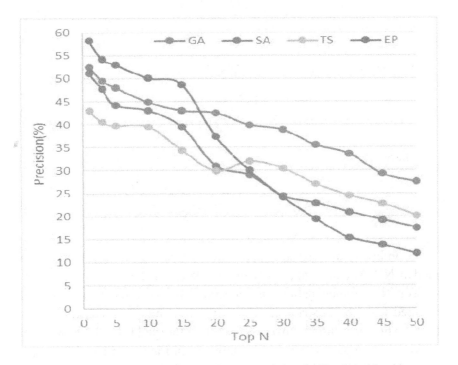

Figure 7.4 Precision Value of Top N Recommendations by Heuristic Algorithms

7.2.2. *Empirical Study 2 - Comparison with Different Recommenders*

In this part, we compare the performance of our proposed MLaaS approaches, empowered by EP and GA, with other widely used recommenders in cold start problem.

A user-based recommender is retrieved by predicting user rating (preference) with:

$$P_{u,j}^{U} = \frac{\sum sim^{U}(i,j)(P_{u,i}^{U} - \overline{P_{i}^{U}})}{\sum sim^{U}(i,j)} \tag{7.3}$$

where:

$$sim^{U}(i,j) = \frac{\sum_{u \in U}(P_{u,i}^{U} - \overline{P_{i}^{U}})(P_{u,j}^{U} - \overline{P_{j}^{U}})}{\left|\sum_{u \in U}(P_{u,i}^{U} - \overline{P_{i}^{U}})\right|\left|\sum_{u \in U}(P_{u,j}^{U} - \overline{P_{j}^{U}})\right|} \tag{7.4}$$

An item-based recommender is also built according to:

$$P_{u,j}^{I} = \frac{\sum sim^{I}(u,w)P_{w,j}^{I}}{\sum sim^{I}(u,w)} \tag{7.5}$$

where

$$sim^{I}(u,w) = \frac{\sum_{L_{j} \in L}(P_{u,j}^{I} - \overline{P_{j}^{I}})(P_{w,j}^{I} - \overline{P_{j}^{I}})}{\left|\sum_{L_{j} \in L}(P_{u,j}^{I} - \overline{P_{j}^{I}})\right|\left|\sum_{L_{j} \in L}(P_{w,j}^{I} - \overline{P_{j}^{I}})\right|} \tag{7.6}$$

In addition, we also apply two well-established similarity measure models NHSM (Liu et al., 2014) and ACOS (Ahn, 2008).

Top N recommendations are generated by these recommenders. As inspired from the experiment 1, we set N as continuous integers from 1 to 20, which is a little bit over the potential threshold, 15. Take the N as x-axis, the comparison results are shown as in Figure 7.5 and 7.6. Please note the GA and EP represent genetic algorithm and evolutionary programming.

Top N recommendations are generated by these recommenders. As inspired from the experiment 1, we set N as continuous integers from 1 to 20, which is a little bit over the potential threshold, 15. Take the N as x-axis, the comparison results are shown as in Figure 7.5 and 7.6. Please note the GA and EP represent genetic algorithm and evolutionary programming.

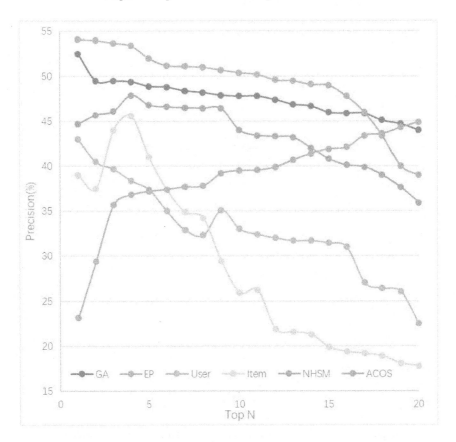

Figure 7.5 Precision Values of Top N Results by Different Recommenders

From Figure 7.5, it is found that, although ACOS produces better recommendations after the N is larger than 18 in terms of the Precision values, its initial recommendation quality is comparatively poor. The experiment shows the authors' finding was correct that adopting NHSM could improve the performance of user-based and also item-based recommenders significantly (Liu et al., 2014). However, GA-based and EP-based MLaaS approaches can generate results with higher precisions than NHSM overall, regardless the size of N (N≤20).

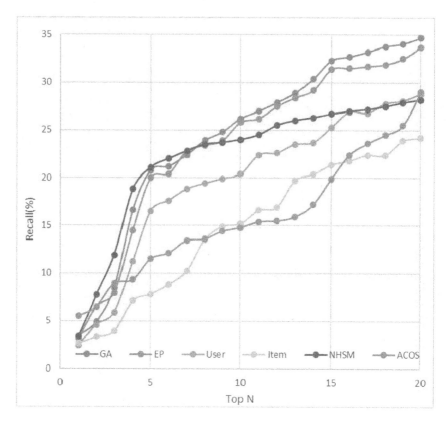

Figure 7.6 Recall Values of Top N Results by Different Recommenders

As aforementioned, generally in judging the qualities of a micro OER recommendation, the Precision value comes before the Recall values. If we observe the Recall values produced by these selected recommenders as well (Figure 7.6), the NHSM generates best results when N is less than 5 and then it falls to lower than GA-based and EP-based MLaaS approach, and the respective differences are both expanded along with the increasing value of N. Aside from this, although ACOS is the only one recommender with both ascending Recall and Precise values, its upcurve is below the NHSM's until N=20. It is noteworthy that, at the potential threshold (i.e., N=15), the other recommenders' performance on retrieving relevant micro OERs from all candidates cannot compete with GA-based and EP-based MLaaS approaches'. Hence, combining both

Precision and Recall values, and considering together with the findings in the Experiment 1, the final winner still goes to either the GA-based or the EP-based approach. Case by case, the algorithm selection depends on the specific requirement of recommendations. Generally, GA is a more stable choice, while EP has strength in accuracy.

In summary, the proposed online computation of MLaaS is feasible to deal with new user cold start problem in micro OER recommendation, by producing optimal results with acceptable Recall and Precision values. Some widely-used recommenders do not consider learning distraction, resulting in their lower qualities of responses on cold start by only considering user ratings. Among all heuristic algorithms used, EP and GA stand out and the suggestive size of the recommendation list is 15.

7.2.3. Learning Path Evaluation

To demonstrate the effectiveness of the proposed solution for new item cold start problem, in this section we evaluate the qualities of generated learning path with newly published micro OERs inserted. We borrow the concept of 10-cross validation, by dividing the micro OERs in the relevant fields into two portions, in a ratio of 1:9. Learning paths were generated among the nine-tenth micro OERs. For each learning path, one micro OER from the rest is selected and treated as newly published micro OERs in the experiment. The Algorithm 6.4 is executed to find a place for each new member to the majority. The Figure 7.7 gives the violation degree (i.e. *VD* as defined in the Section 6.2.1) for the learning paths with new micro OERs inserted generated by using MLaaS approach against those generated by using the shortest-path approach (Alian and Jabri, 2009) and competency-based approach (Hsu and Li, 2015).

In total, 3674 micro OERs in the information technology field, 4479 micro OERs in the business field and 3254 in the social science field are picked up as candidates; and 366, 448 and 325 of them were selected out as test items, respectively. After the execution of the Algorithm 6.4, in the information technology field 2044 new learning paths come out, while in the business and social science fields the numbers are 3746 and 2329. This is because one or more places are found for a new micro

OERs; or according to the Algorithm 6.4, two new learning paths are generated when there is a 'RecommendedSequence' relation. The shortest-path (SP) approach and competency-based (C-based) approach are executed as well to put newly published micro OERs into places among or in parallel with items in established learning paths. Actually, the working principles of SP and C-based are not finding a place for the newly published micro OER within the established learning path, but rebuilding a new learning path thoroughly.

According to the Figure 7.7, the average violation degrees of the learning paths generated separately by the three approaches are compared in terms of the three disciplines. It can be found that MLaaS approach outperforms SP and C-based approach overall, as average *VDs* of MLaaS-generated learning paths in each discipline are far less than the others. Also, the SP approach is difficult to identify a reasonably learning path provided that there are many micro OERs loosely correlated (i.e. with the weak order RecommendedSequence).

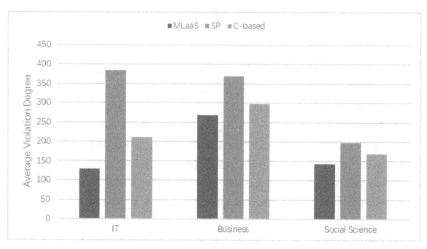

Figure 7.7 Performance Comparison of 3 Approaches – Average Violation Degrees of All Generated Learning Paths

Afterwards, we evaluate the best solutions that are produced by MLaaS, SP and C-based. Therein, one test micro OER is only allowed to be involved in one learning path; and for each test object, the new learning path with lowest *VD* value is selected. This is to eliminate the potential influences brought by the loose coupling of prior/posterior micro OER pairs. In this case, the amount of the nominated learning paths exactly equals to the amount of test micro OERs, namely 366, 448 and 325, respectively.

The results in the Figure 7.8 show same observations that the MLaaS approach surpasses the other two approaches, by finding better places to insert newly published micro OERs meanwhile breaking the rules (as described in the subsection B of Section 6.2.1) less times. It is worth noting that the average violation difference is considerably larger in the information technology discipline. This is probably because the learning paths in this field are relatively longer. In other words, an individual learning path that goes through a complete information technology knowledge area consists of more micro OERs than those of business and social science. In addition, all of the three approaches produce learning paths with higher violation degrees in the business discipline. It can be potentially attributed to that micro OERs having other OERs as knowledge pre-requirement, and one micro OER being closely related to more than one of the others, are more often found in the business discipline.

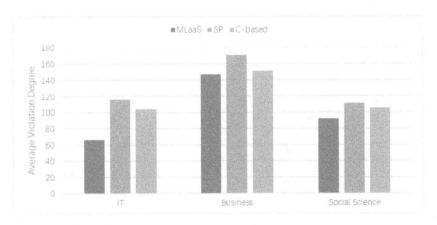

Figure 7.8 Performance Comparison of 3 Approaches – Average Violation Degrees of the Best Learning Paths for Each Test Micro OER

Summary

In this Chapter, the system implementation and empirical evaluation of algorithms were presented. In the Section 7.1, we demonstrated the topology of this system, for which a peer-to-cloud-peer structure was adopted to facilitate the file transmission. In conjunction of services in the offline computation domain, the Adaptive Engine makes decision to allocate adaptive micro OERs to learners. Its working principle was shown in a process diagram, in the Figure 7.2.

The Section 7.2 presented the empirical evaluation of our proposed approaches, for both new user and new item cold start problems. Results showed that GA and EP were suggested to be adopted as the core algorithm in the computation for new learner cold start problem. The both heuristic algorithms can improve the performance of some well-developed recommenders. Furthermore, the Algorithm 6.4 is proven to be able to find more appropriate places in established learning paths for newly published micro OERs.

Chapter 8

Conclusion

8.1 Summary

8.1.1. *Research Background Review*

It is gradually common that learning resources can be accessed via mobile devices. As a completely new form, the appearance of m-learning has lifted the traditional ways of learning resource delivery in distance learning, while learning on-the-move brings in remarkable challenges for both learners and learning resource providers to settle in this new learning context. It is worth noting that even the m-learning itself is evolving year by year, while learning behaviours varies all the way according to the change of space and time. Among these changes, an obvious difference from the traditional mobile learning is that the average length for each learning activity becomes fragmented. In other words, more and more learning activities are carried out within a relatively short time span, which is generally less than 15 minutes.

Building on the trend of open learning, the delivery of OER is recognized as a novel and effective approach that leads to a revolution to the traditional way of learning. OERs are 'digital learning resources offered online freely and openly to teachers, educators, students, and independent learners in order to be used, shared, combined, adapted, and expanded in teaching, learning, and research.' (Hylen et al., 2012). OER providers and instructors have leveraged mobile devices for learners to easily participate in learning activities, regardless of restrictions in time and location. However, as micro-learning evolves, micro-content delivery with a sequence of micro interactions enables users to learn without being inhibited by information overload (Guo et al., 2015).

133

Effective micro-content delivery is a key technology for ensuring better learning results in terms of cognitive retention of content in learners' minds. Traditional pedagogical approaches and syllabi clearly require high levels of adaptation to apply to such a completely new educational environment.

8.1.2. Mobile Learning

In this book we have introduced a research on facilitating micro open learning in mobile environment. This approach is towards providing adaptive OERs in the form of micro learning resources, which are fragmented pieces tailored to fulfil the requirement of learning in short time spans and in mobile environments.

This research commenced by a comprehensive literature review, which crossed the fields of information technology, pedagogy and social science. This work was presented in the Chapter 2. Having been adopted for years, the features of distance learning and its development was discussed in the Chapter 2.1. The wide use of mobile devices brought mobile learning to a major mode in distance learning, and the new shape of it, namely micro learning, gained its popularity very quickly in recent years. Their features were introduced in the same section as well. Open learning, together with its shapes, instructional design and benefit were investigated in the Section 2.2, and the feasibility of embracing service-oriented architecture with the OER delivery was also touched. Consequently, this book discovered the impacts and advantages of the combination of the micro learning and open learning in the Section 2.3. To realize the adaptive micro OER delivery, there are a variety of learning technologies and research approaches involved, which were rolled out in the Section 2.4. this book illustrated the theoretical background and existing studies over the learner modelling, educational data mining and analytics, and big data in education.

Inspired by the issues concluded from the literature review, the Chapter 3 focused on how to design the research to improve the micro open learning context and offer learners better learning experience so as to achieve better outcomes. The design started from the research background identification and introduction of previous work, which can be found in the Section 3.1. Our pilot study motivated us to facilitate the current delivery shape of OER, by bringing in the adaptive micro learning concept. Meanwhile, for the first decision-making process in micro OER adaptation, we were motivated to organize an online computation, which aimed to tackle the famous cold start problem. This is illustrated in the Section 3.2. Consequently, research challenges in terms of micro OER delivery, online computation and cold start problem were summarized in order. How to address these research challenges were illustrated in the Section 3.4, where the anticipated outcomes and example scenarios of adaptive micro OER delivery were presented. Following it, we proposed the system framework of MLaaS, for both offline and online computation, in the Section 3.5.

A comprehensive learner model was conceptually built in the Chapter 4. It consists of factors from the internal and external domains. Differentiated by the relevance to the learners' cognitive and intellectual levels, intellectual and non-intellectual factors were pickup in the internal domain. A component can belong to more than one domains and different components can be associated, in which case they are shown as overlapped in the Figure 4.1. From the learning content perspective, according to the availabilities from the open learning provider, there are ready-made micro OERs and Non-micro OERs. Both types of OERs are subject to categorization and customization, and a mechanism was set up to measure their functional and non-functional attributes. The details of the micro open learning content profiling can be found in the Section 4.2.

The Chapter 5 focused on the construction of a semantic knowledge base, which underpins the decision-making process executed by the Adaptive Engine in the offline computation domain. The knowledge base was built in a two-tier structure, with a pattern level at the top and a data level at the bottom. Two augmented ontologies, respectively for micro OER and micro learning content, were settled based on conceptual graphs at the pattern level. Subsequently, a data processing strategy was designed at the data level, where an EDM and LA based approach was proposed towards understanding patterns and rules in micro learning. In the same section (i.e. Section 5.2.3), the data sources were also demonstrated from the on-campus and open learning perspectives.

In the Chapter 6, this book constructed an online computation, which works against the sparsity of data at the commencement of micro open learning, and for real-time learner model updating. Most importantly, it contains a solution to solve the cold start problem in the micro OER recommendation caused by the shortage and brevity of learner information and the newly published micro OERs. A lightweight learner-micro OER profile was established in terms of learner preference propagation, distraction prediction and instant time availability identification, while a heuristic algorithm based approach produced the optimized computational recommendations for the new learner cold start problem. In addition, another heuristic algorithm enhanced by Hill Climbing was presented to find places in established learning paths for newly published micro OERs. In the Section 6.3, real-time complementary mechanisms were introduced to keep the comprehensive learner model up-to-date and enable the responses to learners being in second granularities.

The Chapter 7 contained the system implementation and empirical evaluation of algorithms. The topology setting of the system borrowed the idea of peer-to-cloud-peer where a layer of p2p network was organized among leaners. It has the advantage that resource transmission can be organized in an easier and faster way. The working principle of the Adaptive Engine was shown in the Section 7.1.2. The workflow was realized by collaborations among a few services in the offline computation domain. In the Section 7.2 experiments were conducted to identify the heuristic algorithms with better performance; and the selected algorithms, GA and EA, were compared with well-developed recommenders simulated from literature.

8.2 Recommendation for Future Work

8.2.1. *Cross Learning Problem*

For in-progress micro-learning where students learn fragmented content from various sources, considerations regarding the alignment of ontologies, which come from hundreds of OER providers, should be taken seriously because there is not any common semantic standard among them. It is often observed that learners repeatedly switch among OERs offered by different institutions. These OERs may offer the same topics, but they are delivered in different ways with different pedagogies. Consequently, learners are free to choose the content and to combine this content in different ways to achieve the outcomes they desire. In addition, some OER learners do not have a concrete aim to acquire the specific knowledge; rather, they are completing an entire course merely to obtain the credits. They may need to engage themselves in some small course units offered by different OER providers. Therefore, a novel mechanism is crucial to support learning across institutions. Subsequently, the practice of the exchange and reuse of OERs among different providers has emerged, which brings up the problem of ontology interoperability. While many e-learning metadata standards and user-defined metadata exist, they still lack formal semantics. The semantic Web technologies provide ontology for organizations to annotate learning resources semantically into learning objects to facilitate knowledge sharing and re-use by others. Different ontologies can use different e-learning metadata to describe the same or similar sets of learning objects. The related learning objects dispersed over a heterogeneous learning resource system are still difficult to discover and re-use within other courseware.

Given the adaptive micro open learning has been activated successfully by leveraging the solution for cold start as presented in the Chapter 6, the second problem the learner might be facing in the learning path would be the cross-learning problem. The interoperability of cross-institute ontologies has to be improved.

It is anticipated that all micro OER chunks will be annotated with ontologies into learning objects. These ontologies contain those newly established in the construction of semantic learner model and learning resource profiling; and the existing ones, which used different metadata standards, which are extracted from OER providers. All ontologies will be placed in a pool, and a semantic ontology mapping approach will be developed to deal with the semantic and structural heterogeneity. New techniques will also be proposed to detect both conflicts. A bridging ontology will also be proposed to act as a core to generate mapping rules, which reconciles terms defined in the OER ontology pool with terms defined in the target ontology, which have been agreed upon by various OERs.

8.2.2. System Prototyping

Our future research will concentrate on carrying out EDM and LA over identified data sources available from data warehouse of Australian universities. The machine learning-based approach will be selected and evaluated to train data in order to produce the semantically constructed learner model, which was introduced as in the Chapter 4. This model will be stored in the offline domain and updated by the offline and online domains in conjunction.

We will also put in efforts on the rule discovery and combine its results with the learner model. These findings will be provided into the Adaptive Engine as input to infer learners' profiles in the offline computation. Feasible artificial intelligence-based solutions will be developed accordingly to achieve the ultimate goal, which is to match the learners' needs with the most suitable learning resource. Furthermore, computational intelligence methods will be adopted to optimize the determination of learning paths for learners.

The system will be programmatically prototyped and deployed over the Amazon Web Service as demonstrated in the Chapter 7.

8.2.3. Case Study Design

At present, besides tests or exams, there is a lack of effective approaches to assess what and how much learners have actually achieved from open learning, so that a quantitative research is needed to investigate their satisfaction towards learning process and progress periodically.

The key questions of the upcoming case study are to evaluate 'whether learners can enjoy micro open learning through micro learning manner' and 'how micro learning can influence learners' knowledge acquisition'. To answer these questions, we will test our system with a pilot study and formulate the following hypotheses as listed in the Table 8.1.

Table 8.1 Hypotheses about Micro Learning Experience and Knowledge Acquisition

H1	*Participating in open learning activities by accessing small unit of customized learning resource has positive impacts on learners to assimilate and internalize specific knowledge while avoiding obtaining interference information*
H2	*Micro OERs in the form of visual information are easier for learners to memorize or internalize in short durations.*
H3	*Adaptive learning resources with personal tailoring help learner to conduct effective time management so as to contribute to fulfilling the requirements of entire course learning.*
H4	*Learners who do not intend to get course credits have higher satisfaction on micro learning experience than hour-long learning.*
H5	*Micro learning contents with concrete time restrictions are better for learners to acquire targeted knowledge. Failing to complete a course unit at a time can result in information missing.*
H6	*Simple types of course assessment, such as quiz, multiple choice, etc., are suggested to be finished in micro learning units, which can timely provide refresher and knowledge review for learners, and then help to fix it in memories deeply.*

Data from behaviours over fragmented learning resources will be collected to test the above hypotheses. We will also carry out case studies focusing on finding out how our proposed system can facilitate micro learning in MOOC and how it can, qualitatively and quantitatively, help learners achieve their learning expectations. It is suggested to initiate interviews as well as surveys of engaged learners to collect data and analyse the main aspects of feedback. Also, evaluations will be carried out to test the usefulness and ease of use of the proposed system.

way. Open learning has resided in public domain and been organized under licenses for free use and any other reuse and repurposing (Harley, 2008).

Open learning seeks to remove all unnecessary barriers to learning, while aiming to provide students with a reasonable chance of success in an education and training system centred on their specific needs and located in multiple arenas of learning (Neil Butcher, 2011). It incorporates several key principles:

- Learning opportunity should be lifelong and should encompass both education and training (Leone, 2018);
- The learning process should be centred on the learners, build on their experience and encourage independent and critical thinking (Hannafin et al., 2013);
- Learning provision should be flexible so that learners can increasingly choose, where, when, what and how they learn, as well as the pace at which they will learn;
- Prior learning, prior experience and demonstrated competencies should be recognized so that learners are not unnecessarily restricted from educational opportunities by lack of appropriate qualifications;
- Learners should be able to load progress or accumulate credits from different learning contexts;
- Providers should create the conditions for a fair chance of learner success.

Resources used in open learning are ranging from full courses, course materials, modules, textbooks, streaming videos, tests, software, and any other tools, materials, or techniques used to support access to knowledge (Atkins et al., 2007). Formally, OERs are 'digital learning resources offered online freely and openly to teachers, educators, students, and independent learners in order to be used, shared, combined, adapted, and expanded in teaching, learning and research' (Hilton, 2016). Researchers summarized the development of OER conforms with a '5R', wherein, the 'Retain' refers to 'make and own copies', the 'Reuse' indicates 'use in a wide range of ways', 'Revise' represents the action of 'adapt, modify and improve', 'Remix' equals to 'combine two or more' and 'share with others' is highlighted by 'Redistribute' (Theeraroungchaisri, 2016).

The following issues mainly account for the speedy development and wide acceptance of the open learning, or, in other words, the utilization of OER.

- Cost: the problem of cost (e.g. for textbooks) comes always at the first place to the user/customer side in the e/m-learning even traditional on-campus learning, where these customers can be either the learners or the education providers. This problem is exposed more significant in developing counties (Lesko, 2013).

- License: Copyright restrictions on textbooks, journals, and other educational objects prevent educators from combining materials in a way that best meets the demands of their students. It also reduces the feasibility to break and re-construct learning resources from different institutions.

- Local Support: Although OER is fully international; there were needs for local support. Chae and Jenkins (2015) summarized from their participants' opinion that they are delighted to have a local OER service unit on campus and a readily available person who are well versed in finding, utilizing, designing and tailoring of OER. These go-to persons help incoming instructional designers, instructors and other stakeholders in open learning to get familiar with the similar operations on OERs, so that they promote the use of OER in both learning and teaching.

Index

CPSIA information can be obtained
at www.ICGtesting.com
Printed in the USA
BVHW090244260220
573339BV00007B/17

9 789811 207457